BRIGHT NOTES

GULLIVER'S TRAVELS BY JONATHAN SWIFT

Intelligent Education

Nashville, Tennessee

BRIGHT NOTES: Gulliver's Travels
www.BrightNotes.com

No part of this publication may be used or reproduced in any manner whatsoever without written permission, except in the case of brief quotations in critical articles and reviews. For permissions, contact Influence Publishers http://www.influencepublishers.com.

ISBN: 978-1-645422-88-4 (Paperback)
ISBN: 978-1-645422-89-1 (eBook)

Published in accordance with the U.S. Copyright Office Orphan Works and Mass Digitization report of the register of copyrights, June 2015.

Originally published by Monarch Press.
Richard Feingold, 1964
2019 Edition published by Influence Publishers.

Interior design by Lapiz Digital Services. Cover Design by Thinkpen Designs.

Printed in the United States of America.

Library of Congress Cataloging-in-Publication Data forthcoming.
Names: Intelligent Education
Title: BRIGHT NOTES: Gulliver's Travels
Subject: STU004000 STUDY AIDS / Book Notes

CONTENTS

1)	Introduction to Jonathan Swift	1
2)	Introduction to Gulliver's Travels	9
3)	Brief Summary	11
4)	Textual Analysis	
	Book I: A Voyage to Lilliput	27
	Book II	62
	Book III	100
	Book IV	141
5)	Character Analyses	185
6)	Critical Commentary	193
7)	Study GuideEssay Questions and Answers	199
8)	Bibliography and Topics for the Research	206

INTRODUCTION TO JONATHAN SWIFT

SWIFT AND GULLIVER'S TRAVELS

Jonathan Swift was an old man already when his masterpiece, *Travels Into Several Remote Nations of the World,* was published in 1726. *Gulliver's Travels*, as the work came to be called, was an immediate popular success but it brought its author neither profit nor joy, and, at sixty years of age, Swift was not concerned with fame; during his long, difficult and frustrating life, he had already acquired what fame he was to enjoy.

Swift was born in Ireland in 1667; he was educated there and spent much of his early life in that country but, for an extended period from 1708 to 1715, he passed an invigorating and exciting part of his life in England, deeply involved in politics and deeply engaged in some of the most exciting and important developments in the history of England at that period. In those eight years, Swift was recognized as one of the most brilliant men of his age, and certainly, as the most brilliant wit of an age renowned for sparkling minds but, in 1715, (when his party fell from power) there was no longer a place for him in England. He returned to Ireland, bitterly disappointed at the turn of political events and bitterly resigned to what seemed to him a life of obscurity as Dean of St. Patrick's Cathedral in Dublin. It was during these years of frustration and despondency, after 1715, that *Gulliver's Travels* was conceived and written. When Swift brought the manuscript with him to England, in 1726, he had not traveled outside of Ireland for eleven years. Those eleven years were not empty for Swift; they were filled with an involvement in Irish life that won for him the love of the Irish people but no real success and no joy. When Swift came to England in 1726, it was a renowned and tormented old man whose great work was as written in the bitter experience of what he considered to be his Irish exile.

SWIFT'S LIFE

Swift's youth was undistinguished. Born into a poor family in 1667, it was arranged that he receive an education but his brilliance was not of the type that distinguishes itself in formal academic studies. He has granted the B.A. as a "special grace" by Trinity College in Dublin. His work itself did not merit the degree. He spent a number of years after his graduation as secretary to a famous nobleman, Sir William Temple. Those were important years in Swift's life for his connection with Temple brought him into the midst of English and Irish political and intellectual life.

Swift followed the usual course open to young men of poor means and great ability: he sought a career in the Church, the Church of England, and it was through the Church that he became involved in politics. Some early writings of his on contemporary political issues were noticed and his services were sought by influential leaders of the Whig party. He produced for them a number of pamphlets which were, in effect, propaganda for their cause.

In the early eighteenth century in England, religion and politics were closely connected areas of concern. One's religious position was closely related to one's political affiliations. Now, in 1708, Swift was sent by his Church to England on a diplomatic mission. He was to negotiate with the government for certain interests of the Irish Church relating to taxes. The issue was rather complicated but it soon became clear to Swift that the Whig ministry then in power was not especially favorable to the interests of the Church in Ireland. Negotiations dragged on with no results and Swift was coming to see that, as a churchman, he had misplaced his political allegiance in his connection with the Whigs. In the meantime, the country was growing disaffected with the Whig ministry and, by 1710, it was clear that the ministry was going to fall. It was at this time that the leader of the Tory faction, Robert Harley, made a number of overtures to Swift, trying to persuade him to lend his services as pamphleteer and propagandist to the Tory cause. When it was clear that Harley's faction was going to replace the Whigs and when Harley furthermore promised Swift that the Church's requests would be granted after the Tories took power, Swift broke with the Whigs and joined with Harley whom he served as an adviser and pamphleteer.

The Tories took power in 1710 and the next five years were certainly the high point in Swift's life. He became one of the most influential figures in the English government. He was, furthermore, deeply committed to the outlook of the Tory party (especially as expressed in its policy toward the Church). Thus, it is easy to imagine that, when the Tories lost power in 1715 at the death of Queen Anne, Swift was deeply disturbed. He regretted, of course, the end of his own political career; and he regretted the necessity for his return to Ireland but, more than this, the Whig triumph in 1715 seemed to Swift to be the triumph of a new and ill considered (perhaps dangerous) philosophy of life.

Swift was to live thirty years longer but these were bitter, frustrated and tragic years. They were years spent in constant and unsuccessful opposition to the policies of a firmly victorious Whig enemy. Swift hated his life in Ireland but he became the first of the great Irish patriots who struggled to save that nation from the economic exploitation and social ruin that seemed to him to be the result of Whig policy in treating Ireland as an English colony.

Though the years after 1715 were years of personal tragedy for Swift, some of his most significant work as a literary artist was done during this period. In 1724, as part of his campaign to prevent the coinage of money in Ireland on terms extremely disadvantageous to the Irish, Swift wrote the brilliant *Drapier's Letters*. These were a series of public letters purportedly written by a simple but clear thinking merchant whose aim was to explain to his countrymen the disastrous effect that the coinage proposal would have on the Irish economy. Of course, the drapier was Swift, the clergyman, and the effect of his letters was to kill the proposal; again, in 1729, Swift, now sixty-three years old, wrote the blistering *Modest Proposal*, the greatest short satirical piece in the English language. Here, Swift put into the mouth of a respectable Whig merchant the chilling proposition that the Irish should fatten their children so that they might serve as food for the tables of the English landlords-and incidentally solve, in this way, the problem of Ireland's rapidly increasing overpopulation. In this way, Swift called attention to the miserable plight of the Irish and he directed his fire against those responsible for that plight. In 1730, Swift wrote his greatest poem, "Verses on the Death of Dr. Swift," a sophisticated and brilliant treatment of the meaning of a man's death to his friends who remain alive. This poem is remarkable for its blend of sophisticated humor and tragic irony. Swift's most fiery, indignant poem, "The Legion Club," was written in 1736. In this poem, he attacks the Irish House of Commons consistently supporting policies which were disastrous to the church. "The Legion Club" is Swift's last notable work. Almost seventy when he wrote it, he was to live on for nine more tormented years, half of them in great physical pain and mental decline, all of them with the awareness that his enemies would continue to prevail.

GULLIVER'S TRAVELS AND THE EARLY EIGHTEENTH CENTURY

The early 18th century in England is often characterized as a period during which the influence of reason and urbanity was most potent. The preceding century had been marked by civil and religious strife but that strife had passed and men looked forward to a life based upon reason and a nation enjoying peace. The religious fanaticism of the past was seen as a nightmare that did not need to be lived through again. The civil warfare of the seventeenth century was over and men hoped to enjoy the benefits of a stable political system based on the rule of law under the system of constitutional monarchy. Hopes were entertained that men would submit to the clear light of reason and it was thought by many that man was naturally good and capable of living the good life through reason.

Now, Swift shared with his time an abhorrence of the bloodshed and fanaticism of the past but he was less optimistic about the natural goodness of man; furthermore, he was skeptical about man's ability to guide his own way through the world according to the dictates of his own reason. In fact,

Swift's was the traditional Christian view of man as a weak, depraved creature who lacked within himself the power to forge for himself the good life. If man was to live well, if man was to protect himself from his own weaknesses and make the best use of his own strengths, he needed the help of religion in the form of an established church and he needed the help of an ordered society within which he knew his place. Therefore, Swift's opposition to the Whigs (for example) stemmed from their antagonism towards the established church, the Church of England. Of course, this was not all, and to say even this much is to make a gross oversimplification. However, Swift's opposition to the Whigs should be seen as more than the expression of mere political partisanship. We should understand, rather, that he felt that the Whig political position was based upon an essentially mistaken notion of the nature of man, the needs of man, and the proper life for man. Thus, when Swift attacks the Whigs he attacks an attitude towards life which he fears is dangerous.

Gulliver's Travels is Swift's great statement in support of the traditional view of man. In this book, we will find an attack leveled against what Swift believed to be mistaken ways of life based upon mistaken views of the nature of man. There will be a great deal of political **satire**. In Book I especially, Swift will be representing satirically many of the events of the years 1708–1715 when the Whigs and Tories struggled for power. In Book III, he will show what happens when too much faith is placed in the ability of the human intellect and, in Book IV, he will shatter any simple notions of the natural goodness of man.

In many ways, *Gulliver's Travels* is a difficult book for us to understand for it challenges many of the basic assumptions of our lives. It challenges science, it disturbs our faith in reason and the natural goodness of man. It is unsympathetic to an economic system based upon finance and technology and, while it extols human freedom, its analysis of the source of that freedom (and the dangers to it) is considerably different from what our analysis would be. That is why *Gulliver's Travels* is so important a book for us today. We live in the modern world and are struggling with unprecedented problems. *Gulliver's Travels* was written as the modern world was being born and Swift was not happy with what he saw coming to pass. He has, therefore, given us a book which helps us measure our achievements, our failures and our predicaments against those of another age and another set of values.

SWIFT'S OTHER WORKS

Swift was a prolific but not a professional writer. He did not write to earn money. Most of his work was political in nature; pamphlets, propaganda and history and, because of the nature of his writings, almost everything he did had to be published anonymously.

The Drapier's Letters and *A Modest Proposal* have been mentioned already. Besides *Gulliver's Travels* and these two works, students will be interested in *A Tale of a Tub*, a brilliant satiric treatment of religious dogmatism and fanaticism. This work was written during Swift's youth and shows an exuberant and ingenious wit that is often hilarious and always piercing. Another work of his youth, *The Battle of the Books*, carries the satiric attack against the pedantry and dogmatism of vain learning. Another famous work, *the Argument Against Abolishing Christianity*, is a brilliantly ironic use of satiric technique to show what it really means to be a Christian and how far indeed men are from living the kind of life they profess to admire.

These are Swift's major works but his total output is much larger and fills many volumes. Much of his remaining work is very topical but hardly dull. It consists of pieces written for *The Examiner*, a forerunner of the modern newspaper. There are works on English history of which the most interesting is an account of the Tory ministry Swift was connected with and there are miscellaneous pieces of all kinds, some light and humorous, some bitter and resigned. Perhaps the most fascinating because of its biographical candor is the Journal to Stella, a day by day account of Swift's experiences in England during the days of the Tory ministry. *The Journal* is fascinating for the personal glimpses it affords into the relationship between Swift and Esther Johnson who was his closest friend and may have been the woman he loved.

GULLIVER'S TRAVELS

INTRODUCTION

A LETTER FROM CAPTAIN GULLIVER TO HIS COUSIN SYMPSON

The reader should not make the mistake of skipping over this introductory letter for it is the real beginning of the book. Swift, of course, has made it seem merely a prefatory note (of the kind we are accustomed to ignore) but he has done this to underscore the reader's conception of Gulliver, rather than Swift, as the true author of the book.

The important thing to recognize in this letter is its chronological relationship to the events of the book proper: the letter is supposedly written on the occasion of the book's publication. This means that the writer of the letter, Gulliver, has been through the experiences we as readers are about to encounter. The letter is therefore important as an indication of the impact his experiences have had on Gulliver.

What we find, as we read the letter, is that it is the work of a bitter man. We notice his carping criticisms of the publisher whom he accuses of tampering with the manuscript. We notice that Gulliver was reluctant to publish his book and did so against his better judgment; but most striking is the author's attitude toward the human race. He has the habit of referring to people in the terms usually reserved for animals: he has a tendency to consider himself apart from the human race and he clearly expresses his disillusionment with and his disgust for man. As we read further, we discover that the author of the letter spends a good deal of his time in his stables conversing with his horses! He mentions this as a matter of fact but the careful reader cannot help recognizing that the writer of the letter, though he has sufficient control over his senses to pen his thoughts, is nevertheless at least partially mad!

The reader's job is now clearly set before him. He must come to the book bearing in mind the fact that the experiences he is to read about have driven the author (the man who lived through those experiences) mad. What then has Gulliver learned about life and mankind that has so affected him? The answer to that question is in the pages to follow: the story of Gulliver's four voyages to remote nations of the world.

GULLIVER'S TRAVELS

BRIEF SUMMARY

BOOK I

Lemuel Gulliver, the son of a Nottinghamshire man of small means, is forced to leave college at Cambridge because his father cannot afford to keep him there. At age of 17, he goes to London and is apprenticed to Mr. James Bates, a surgeon. After four years with Bates, Gulliver goes to Leyden on the continent to continue his medical studies. Returning to England after two years, he gets a position as a ship's surgeon and makes a number of voyages. His ambition, however, is to settle in London and establish a practice there. This he unsuccessfully attempts to do and is soon forced to return to the sea in order to support his wife whom he had married upon his return from a previous voyage.

Gulliver sets out to sea again on board the ship Antelope on May 4, 1699. The ship, however, encounters a violent storm and is destroyed. By some chance, Gulliver finds himself alive as the sole survivor and manages to swim to the shore of a strange land. The exhausted man sinks into a deep sleep as soon as he reaches dry land and awakes to the strangest adventure that has ever yet befallen him. He finds himself bound to the earth by many fine threads so arranged that he cannot move a limb nor turn his head. He soon realizes that he is surrounded by an army of tiny people who are not more than six inches tall!

Gulliver recognizes that it would be foolish to try to struggle free. His first attempt to do so is rewarded by a painful shower of tiny arrows which embed themselves in his face and hands. Momentarily accepting his position as a captive, he is somewhat relieved to discover that the little people, the Lilliputians, have made elaborate arrangements to feed and care for their new guest. He is given food and wine and soon falls into a sleep induced by a drug in the wine. While in his drugged sleep, Gulliver is wheeled to the outskirts of the great city of Lilliput, Mildendo, where he is lodged in an abandoned temple which is barely large enough for him to fit into. He is chained to the building but is given a long enough chain so that he can walk about within a limited area.

The day after his arrival at the Lilliputian capital, Gulliver is visited by the Emperor and his court. The Emperor orders several noted scholars to teach Gulliver the Lilliputian language. Making great progress in the new tongue, Gulliver utters his first request: it is for his freedom. The Emperor admonishes him to be patient and asks the giant to permit his pockets to be searched. Gulliver, not wishing to jeopardize his chances for freedom, willingly assents.

In a short while, the Lilliputians begin to trust Gulliver. He permits the tiny children to play hide and seek in his hair; he allows them to dance in his hands and the Lilliputians, in turn, entertain him by permitting him to watch several of their court diversions. He witnesses the sport of rope dancing, for example, in which a candidate for high government office is forced to balance himself on a rope held six inches from the floor, jump high in the air and then come down standing on the rope. He witnesses another game in which candidates for high honor (symbolized by threads of various colors) are made to leap over and creep under a stick which is raised and lowered at the Emperor's pleasure. So pleased are the Lilliputians with their giant guest that they agree to grant him his freedom. However, for no good reason, Skyresh Bolgolam, the admiral of the realm, has decided to consider Gulliver his enemy. Bolgolam reluctantly agrees with the decision to free Gulliver but insists that Gulliver be forced to abide by a set of nine conditions in return for his freedom. Among these conditions are the following: Gulliver is asked (1) to give two hours warning before entering the capital city, (2) to serve as the Emperor's messenger, (3) to survey the Emperor's domains and (4) not to leave the country without official permission. Gulliver agrees to these terms although he feels that not all of them are honorable.

Soon after receiving his freedom, Gulliver is visited by Reldresal; an important figure in the government. Reldresal briefs Gulliver on certain aspects of Lilliputian political history. Gulliver learns that the Lilliputians are divided against themselves politically and religiously. There are two political factions: the High Heels and the Low Heels. These correspond to two religious factions: the Big-Endians and Little-Endians. One's membership in one or the other of these factions depends upon whether he breaks his eggs on the large or small end. Since the time of the present Emperor's grandfather (who ordered that all true believers break their eggs on the small end) these two groups have been mortal enemies. Presently, the Big-Endians are in exile in the neighboring kingdom of Blefuscu and are planning to invade Lilliput with the help of the Blefuscudian Emperor. Reldresal asks Gulliver to help in repulsing the invasion by seizing the Blefuscudian fleet.

Gulliver designs a stratagem by which he is able to attach threads to the fifty Blefuscudian warships and draw them away with him to Lilliput. This he succeeds in doing, although the Blefuscudian sailors manage to hit him with showers of arrows let loose from their bows.

Upon his successful return to Lilliput, Gulliver is given the title of Nardac, the highest honor the Lilliputian Emperor can bestow upon his subjects. However, it is at this point that relations begin to deteriorate between Gulliver and the Emperor. The Emperor, ambitious for power, is not satisfied that Gulliver has destroyed the Blefuscudian war fleet; he now demands that Gulliver destroy the merchant fleet as well, thus ruining Blefuscudian commerce and making Blefuscu a mere colony of Lilliput. Gulliver is horrified at the Emperor's request and refuses to comply with it.

For some time now, Bolgolam's jealousy of and hatred for Gulliver has been growing; nor is Bolgolam the only official who despises the giant. Chief among the other of Gulliver's secret enemies is Flimnap, Treasurer of the Realm, who has long suspected, with absolutely no grounds, that Gulliver is his wife's lover. Now, noticing that the Emperor grew displeased with Gulliver when the giant refused to subjugate the Blefuscudians, Flimnap and Bolgolam fan the fires of the Emperor's rage. The three plot against Gulliver, accusing him of treason, and condemning him to death. At the urging of Redresal, the sentence is made more lenient; Gulliver is to have his eyes put out instead of being executed. However, it remains the secret intention of the plotters to kill Gulliver. They plan to starve him to death gradually after he has been blinded.

Fortunately, Gulliver hears about the plot from an unidentified friend of his. He immediately makes arrangements to flee from Lilliput and go to Blefuscu. He manages to do this although it violates one of the conditions of his freedom, namely, that he may not leave the country without official permission.

At Blefuscu, Gulliver is warmly greeted. The Blefuscudian Emperor and court treat Gulliver very kindly and heartily respond to his pleas for help in outfitting a lifeboat he found onshore. Gulliver works on his boat for a month making it seaworthy. During this time, the Lilliputian Emperor has sent orders to the Blefuscudians to send Gulliver back to Lilliput. The orders, of course, are not followed.

As Gulliver prepares for departure, the Emperor of Blefuscu gives him many gifts. Gulliver is careful to take a number of Blefuscudian cattle and sheep in his pockets.

BOOK II: A VOYAGE TO BROBDINGNAG

Gulliver sets out on his next voyage on June 20, 1702 aboard the ship Adventure commanded by Captain John Nicholas. However, it is not long before the ship runs into trouble; it encounters a violent storm and is driven off course. Finally, land is sighted, and a search party, led by Gulliver, is sent ashore to try to get water for the ship. When the men reach the island, they split up going in different directions. Gulliver walks inland along a dirt road but, after an hour's time, is able to discover nothing. He returns to the shore but is amazed to discover that the rest of the party is rowing frantically back to the ship, pursued by an enormous giant some sixty feet tall.

Gulliver is horrified to realize that he is stranded but he collects his thoughts and once again trudges inland along the same road he used formerly. This time it is not long before he comes upon a number of the giant folk of this new land. They are working on a farm, reaping the barley. Just as one of the workers is about to step on him, Gulliver cries out, surprising the giant, who picks him up, examines him carefully and squeamishly and brings him to his master, the owner of the farm.

Gulliver tries to make the farmer understand that he is a rational creature and not some tiny insect. Not quite sure of what Gulliver actually is, the farmer brings the little man home to his wife who immediately faints, much the way an English lady would faint at the sight of a mouse. Gulliver's dignity is quite wounded.

Soon, however, the farmer's household comes to understand that their new guest is indeed a little man. They treat him as kindly as possible but his new environment is a great trial for him. In the course of a few hours, he is almost killed by the baby of the house who puts Gulliver in his mouth; he is attacked by two rats, which are, in Brobdingnag, the size of huge hounds and he is threatened by the family cat. However, Gulliver is able to outface that beast although she is the size of an elephant.

In the farmer's family is his daughter, a nine-year-old girl named Glumdalclitch. She is taken with an immediate fondness for the little man and is overjoyed when he is placed in her care. Glumdalclitch indeed treats Gulliver with loving kindness, as if he were her baby. She gives him the nickname Grildrig.

The farmer's friends are amazed to see the strange little man; he becomes the center of attention when the farmer has visitors. It is not long, therefore, before the farmer conceives the idea of displaying Gulliver publicly in order to earn money. Indeed, the farmer takes his little captive into town one day and scores such a huge success with the crowds that he decides to take Gulliver on a tour of the major cities of the kingdom, stopping in each in order to display the little man. Accordingly, the farmer, his daughter, another servant and Gulliver set out together to tour Brobdingnag.

The tour, however, is a great strain on Gulliver's health. He begins to waste away and is near death. The farmer, fearing that his showpiece will die, makes him work all the harder; intending, in this way, to make as much money as possible while Gulliver remains alive.

This is the state of affairs when the troupe enters Lorbrulgrud, the metropolis of Brobdingnag. Soon news of the amazing little man reaches the ears of the queen. Gulliver is brought to her and she is charmed by him. Indeed, she is so pleased that she offers to buy him from the farmer who readily agrees to the transaction thinking that Gulliver has very little time to live. Gulliver, as might be expected, is not sorry at this turn of events. He is particularly happy that Glumdalclitch is to remain with him as his nurse since he has developed quite a bit of affection for her because of her kindness to him.

Gulliver's life at court is an improvement over his existence with the farmer but it is a trying time for him nonetheless. The world of Brobdingnag is simply too large for him. He is constantly threatened by flies; the court monkey almost kills him and the queen's dwarf, who is thirty feet tall, is a constant source of dangerous harassment. However, the queen does what she can to make Gulliver's life bearable. For example, she has a large basin built for him which he has filled with water, and within which he may row a boat. In this way, he is able to exercise while the Queen is delighted to see her little man enjoying himself.

Gulliver has a number of conversations with the King; a wise and just man who thinks very little of what Gulliver has to tell him about life in Europe and England. Gulliver struggles manfully to alter the King's opinion but to no avail. In fact, the more he struggles, the more ridiculous and prideful he seems. Clearly, his sojourn in Brobdingnag is damaging to Gulliver's ego.

While he had been at court, Gulliver had been carried about in a little box about ten feet square. It is in this traveling box that Gulliver accompanies the King and Queen on a journey to a city along the Brobdingnagian seashore. One day, Gulliver pleads with Glumdalclitch to permit him to go to the shore. Glumdalclitch is not well so she reluctantly permits a young boy, a servant, to take Gulliver to the beach. The boy brings Gulliver in his box to the beach and negligently runs off to play by himself. Suddenly Gulliver feels a strong jerk and, as he looks out the window of his box, he realizes that his box, with him in it, is flying high in the air, held in the beak of an eagle. Soon, two other birds give chase and the eagle is forced to drop the box. Gulliver prepares to die but is miraculously saved when his box lands in the ocean.

He soon realizes that his box is being tugged. In an hour's time, he is hauled, within his box, onto an English ship. Gulliver is exhausted by his adventures and furthermore appears to be a madman, telling wild stories about a land of giants sixty feet tall. Not until Gulliver shows the captain several objects from his box, does anybody believe him. Especially remarkable is the tooth of a Brobdingnagian footman; Gulliver gives this item, which is twelve inches long, to the captain as a gift.

After an uneventful voyage, Gulliver reaches England on June 3, 1706. He has been away about four years, two of which have been spent in the land of the giants.

BOOK III: A VOYAGE TO LAPUTA

After his return from Brobdingnag, Gulliver is at home only ten days when he receives another offer to go to sea. It is a good offer and he accepts it. On August 5, 1706, he sets sail aboard the ship Hopewell.

Upon reaching Tonquin, in Indo-China, the captain finds it necessary to lie at anchor for a few months. In order to defray the expense of the voyage during this period, he hires a sloop, puts Gulliver in command and sends it off on a trading voyage. Gulliver's voyage is quite successful at first but he runs into difficulties when he is attacked by two pirate ships simultaneously. One of the ships has, as a crew member, a violent Dutchman who bitterly refuses to heed Gulliver's pleas for mercy. The cruelty of the Dutchman is the more remarkable when it is contrasted with the behavior of the captain of the other pirate ship, a Japanese. Had the Dutchman had his way, all of the crew of Gulliver's sloop would have been murdered; the Japanese captain, however, intercedes and orders that Gulliver be set adrift in a canoe with four days provisions while the rest of the crew is held captive on the two pirate ships.

Accordingly, Gulliver is set adrift. He steers his canoe towards a clump of islands which looms in the distance and reaches it in a few hours. He spends the next few days exploring all of the islands. On the fourth day, while he is walking in the sun, he suddenly perceives that the air grows cooler and the sky darker. He looks up and is amazed to see approaching him an enormous floating object! There are people swarming all over this island in the sky and it is not long before Gulliver is lifted on to it.

As he climbs aboard the flying island, Gulliver is struck with the sight of the strangest people he has ever seen. They are absurdly dressed in long robes studded with figures of the sun, moon, stars and planets. They are amazingly absent minded and constantly falling into spells of deep thought; indeed, so absent minded are they that they cannot carry on conversations without the aid of special servants called "flappers." These flappers gently strike or "flap" the ears of their master when it is his turn to listen, and his mouth when it is his turn to answer. Without the help of these servants, the absent minded inhabitants of the flying island of Laputa would not remember to listen or speak. Other strange customs of the Laputans include the preparation of their food in the shapes of musical instruments and geometrical figures.

Gulliver discovers that this flying island is the abode of a race of mathematicians, astronomers and musicians. He discovers also that these scientists and intellectuals are so far removed from life that their wives despise them, try to escape from them, and are constantly unfaithful. He learns also that the flying island exerts a despotic sway over the continent below, the land of Balnibarbi. Tiring of life on Laputa, Gulliver asks for and receives permission to visit this continent of Balnibarbi.

Gulliver is let down on Balnibarbi in the vicinity of the chief city of that land, Lagado. Upon visiting that city, Gulliver is struck by the wretched state of the people and the buildings. The people are in the throes of poverty while the buildings are in a state of virtual collapse. As he travels about the countryside, Gulliver sees much the same situation prevailing. He notes that the land is fertile but somehow lying wasted. Only on the estate of Count Munodi is there order and productivity.

Gulliver becomes friendly with Count Munodi and learns, from him, the reasons for the miserable state of the kingdom.

Munodi tells Gulliver that agriculture, architecture, learning, and politics are directed by a group known as Projectors, men who are deeply influenced by the abstract learning of the Flying Island and who attempt to apply that learning to the practical problems of running a nation. In the process, the Projectors have virtually ruined the country of Balnibarbi. Munodi himself is in great disfavor with the Projectors because he resists their schemes; they do not seem to be aware that his estate is beautifully kept and productive. They would rather give up his successful methods and adopt their new and impractical procedures.

Gulliver visits the Academy of Projectors and is amazed by the impractical and foolish schemes those men devote their lives to devising. One of them, for example, is attempting to extract sunbeams from cucumbers: another tries to convert human excrement back into the food from which it came, while yet a third is trying to develop a breed of naked sheep. Gulliver tours the entire Academy and is convinced that it is a kind of madhouse.

Gulliver leaves the land of Balnibarbi and visits the island of Glubbdubbdrib. This is a land governed by a magician who has the power to summon up spirits from the past. Gulliver asks the magician to summon the spirits of the classical past and those of modern Europe. By conversing with these ghosts, Gulliver is struck by the inferiority of the modern world as compared to the world of the ancients and is horrified by the cruelty and crime which comprise the saga of human history.

Leaving Glubbdubbdrib, Gulliver next voyages to the island of Luggnagg. He is struck by the despotic attitude of the King of that land whose custom it is to require all visitors to crawl toward him on their bellies while licking the floor with their tongues. However, despite his despotic demeanor, the King is by no means unfriendly. In fact, he is quite pleased with Gulliver's company and offers the Englishman the opportunity to settle permanently in Luggnagg. Gulliver graciously refuses, expressing his desire to return to his wife and family.

Gulliver's most remarkable experience on Luggnagg was his meeting with the Struldbruggs, a race of immortals. When he first heard about them, Gulliver became enraptured at the mere thought of so fortunate a people, a people who lived forever. Imagine his disgust and horror when he met them and discovered that, although they lived forever, they continued to age. When he saw their disgusting bodies and encountered the feebleness of their eternally rotting minds, he realized that death is indeed a boon and that eternal life is a foolish dream for it is worth nothing without eternal youth.

a Taking a cordial leave of the King of Luggnagg, Gulliver sails for Japan where he hopes to find a ship that will take him back to England. The Japanese Emperor is pleasant to Gulliver and, when Gulliver presents him with a letter of introduction from the King of Luggnagg, the Emperor grows quite friendly, so much so, in fact, that he is willing to forego, in Gulliver's case, the custom of forcing his Christian visitor to trample upon the cross. The Emperor warns Gulliver, however, not to tell the Dutch merchants who trade with Japan that he was exempted from this custom. Gulliver is surprised to learned that the heathen Emperor is less concerned that the sacrilegious custom be observed than are the Dutch sailors.

Gulliver is able to secure passage back to Europe on board a Dutch merchant ship. On April 20, 1710, after an absence of five years and six months, he is reunited with his family.

BOOK IV: A VOYAGE TO THE LAND OF THE HOUYHNHNMS

Gulliver is home with his family for only a few months before he once again accepts a most advantageous offer to go to sea, this time as captain of the ship Adventure. On September 7, 1710, he sets sail from Portsmouth. Sickness breaks out among the crew, however, and the ship is forced to put in at Barbados in order to recruit more men. Unfortunately, most of the men who are taken aboard are former criminals and pirates. It is not long before they succeed in debauching the rest of the Gulliver's crew. Soon there is a mutiny. Gulliver is locked in his cabin and carefully guarded. Finally, the leader of the mutineers decides that Gulliver is to be set ashore on a strange and apparently uninhabited island.

The abandoned Gulliver sets about exploring the island after he is left by the crew. He soon encounters an unusually ugly animal whose features roughly resemble those of a hairy human but whose behavior is that of a wild brute. This beast blocks Gulliver's path; the Englishman hits the animal on his arm with the side of his sword causing the brute to set about howling at the top of his lungs. Soon, Gulliver is surrounded by a pack of these beasts who make considerable noise, squirt their excrement all over him and make horrible faces but **refrain** from attacking him.

Suddenly, the pack of brutes scatters in flight. Gulliver cannot tell why; all he sees is the figure of an approaching horse. It is clear, however, that this horse exerts some authority over the ugly brutes. The first horse is soon joined by a second and the two seem to be engaged in rational conversation. As they approach Gulliver, they seem amazed at the sight of him. They examine him carefully, all the while conversing with each other. Gulliver hears them frequently repeat the sound (perhaps a word), "yahoo." He astounds the horses by repeating that word himself. The horses then try to teach him another word, "houyhnhnm," which he is soon able to repeat with little difficulty.

Amazed at his new visitor while his new visitor is no less amazed at him, one of the horses (the grey) leads Gulliver home with him. Gulliver is quite content. If the horses of this island are so reasonable, what paragons of humanity must their masters be! ... such are Gulliver's thoughts. Imagine his amazement then when, upon reaching the abode of what Gulliver takes to be the horse's master, Gulliver discovers that the horse himself is, in fact, the master of the house. Gulliver suddenly realizes that the island itself is ruled by these remarkable horses.

If he is astounded to discover that the horses are the masters of the island, he is dismayed to learn that they consider him to be a "yahoo", which is the name of the ugly brute Gulliver encountered on his arrival on the island. Gulliver does his best to distinguish himself from these brutes but it is not long before he begins to see the resemblance between them and him. When he sees this resemblance, and further when he sees that the yahoos are in every way despicable, his mind begins to totter. He grows disgusted with himself and with the human race and decides to spend the rest of his life with the "Houyhnhnms" ... as the remarkable horses are called. While the yahoos are in every way disgusting, greedy, bellicose and irrational, the noble Houyhnhnms are their exact opposites. Employing the yahoos as servants, the Houyhnhnms live a life of pure reason. Among them are no inordinate and unhealthy ambitions, no disease, no hate, no passion. They are creatures of supreme rationality and Gulliver is dazzled by them.

He has many conversations with his "master" (as he comes to call the grey horse). The result of these talks is to convince Gulliver of the corruption and rottenness of human life and to confirm his decision to live out his life among the Houyhnhnms. Indeed, before a few months are over, he has adapted himself completely to life among the horses. He has outfitted himself with new clothes made from yahoo skin; he has accustomed himself to a diet of milk and oatcakes, and he has resigned himself to living as an inferior creature among beings of dazzling superiority.

Imagine his shock, then, when his master informs him that a council of Houyhnhnms has decided that he must be put off the island! The Houyhnhnms fear that he will corrupt the other yahoos and are adamant in their decision that he must leave. Gulliver faints upon hearing this news but realizes that an edict of the Houyhnhnms is not to be argued against. He sets about building and outfitting a boat and, in two months' time, is ready to depart. As might be expected, the departure is a most painful experience for Gulliver.

Gulliver sails towards an island which looms in the distance. Upon reaching the island, he carefully hides himself so that the savages who inhabit it may not discover him. Soon, however, he is found and his first encounter with humanity, after two years among the Houyhnhnms, is anything but encouraging. The savages pursue him and wound him badly with an arrow in his left knee. So disgusted is he with mankind, however, that when he spies a Portuguese ship in the distance, he decides to forego any chance of rescue to Europe and to take his chances with the savages who almost killed him.

However, the Portuguese discover him and insist that he come aboard their ship. There, he is treated with great kindness by Captain Mendez. However, his two years in Houyhnhnmland have so deranged Gulliver that he is most ungracious towards the captain although he recognizes that Mendez is trying to be very kind. Gulliver's behavior now strikes the reader as the behavior of a madman, so violently is he repelled by the human race.

Captain Mendez persuades Gulliver to return to his wife and family and Gulliver reluctantly agrees. However, as he ends his narrative, we see that is life is far from normal. He tells us that, after being home for five years, he is just now beginning to be able to permit his wife to eat dinner with him. He still cannot abide being touched by her or by any human. In fact, he tells us that he spends the greater part of each day in his stables, conversing quietly with his horses whose smell is far more pleasant to his nostrils than is the odor of his fellow man.

GULLIVER'S TRAVELS

TEXTUAL ANALYSIS

BOOK I: A VOYAGE TO LILLIPUT

INTRODUCTORY NOTE

In this, the first book of the *Travels*, we find a good deal of political allegory and **satire**. Scholars have been able to trace many of the happenings and characters in this section back to a number of significant events and personalities in English politics during the years from about 1708 and 1715. In general, we may consider that Gulliver stands for the Tory faction with which Swift was associated; the Lilliputian intriguers, on the other hand, may be seen to represent Swift's political enemies, the Whigs. The Lilliputian Emperor probably stands for King George I who favored the Whigs. (Professor Arthur Case in *Four Essays on Gulliver's Travels* has treated in detail the political allegory of Book I; the serious student should consult that work.) It would be a mistake, however, to read this first book of the Travels exclusively on the level of political allegory. For one thing, Swift does not provide us with consistent political allegory; it was not his purpose as an artist to supply an exact allegorical representation of a period in England's political history. Therefore, we will find that on occasion the Lilliputian king will behave in a manner which calls to mind the behavior of George I; at other times, we will be able to find no resemblance between the miniature and the real king. Sometimes, we may find Gulliver representing the Tories; at other times, he is simply Lemuel Gulliver. Swift, after all, if he satirizes political corruption in this part of his work, satirizes political corruption in general, not merely as it occurred in England at one particular period of English history. Furthermore, we should not make the mistake of thinking that we have understood the Voyage to Lilliput when we have found, for each of the figures and events in it, a counterpart in English history or in Swift's life. The "Voyage to Lilliput" is about a lot more than Tories and Whigs and political corruption. It is about man. Gulliver will learn something about the nature of man as he associates with the Lilliputians; this section of the Travels should be read as the beginning of the process of Gulliver's awakening to an awareness of what man and life really are.

CHAPTER I

Gulliver introduces himself as the third of five sons of a Nottinghamshire man. His father, a man of small means, nevertheless tried to support his son through school at Emmanuel College, Cambridge. The expenses, however, were too great and Gulliver had to leave school at the age of seventeen after having spent three years there. For four years after leaving school, Gulliver worked as an apprentice to Mr. James Bates, an eminent London surgeon. Completing his apprenticeship to Bates, Gulliver travels to Leyden on the continent and studied medicine there for two years. Upon returning from Leyden, Gulliver took a position as ship's surgeon on a merchant ship,

The Swallow, and set out on a voyage that lasted for three and a half years. Upon his return to London, Gulliver was helped by his old master, Bates, to set up his own practice as a physician. It was at this time that Gulliver married and settled down; his wife is the former Mary Burton.

For two years Gulliver pursued his practice in London, but not successfully. He found it necessary to go to sea again, and, for the next six years, was employed on two ships and made several voyages to the East and West Indies. Tiring of the sea after this long spell, Gulliver returned to London, hoping to pursue his career as a physician successfully but, again, he ran into difficulty and was forced to return to the sea. The story proper begins when Gulliver accepts an offer to sail with Captain William Prichard, master of the ship Antelope. On May 4th, 1699, the Antelope sets sail from Bristol, bound for the south seas.

At first, the voyage is quite successful but, as the ship is en route to the East Indies, it encounters a furious storm; driven by a wild wind, the ship founders upon a rock and splits apart. Gulliver and six others manage to get into a lifeboat but this, too, is soon overturned. Gulliver swims as best he can and, just as he is about to give up the struggle, he finds himself within his depth. He is now able to walk to shore which he reaches at about eight in the evening. Discovering no sign of houses or inhabitants, the exhausted man lies down on the ground and falls into a deep sleep. Apparently, he is the lone survivor of the shipwreck.

When Gulliver awakens, he reckons that he has slept about nine hours; for dawn is just beginning to break. He tries to struggle to his feet but is alarmed to discover that he cannot move. Evidently, he has been tied down to the ground in such a way that he cannot raise his body nor turn his head. Trying to think of a course of action, he grows uneasy as he feels something moving up his left leg. He becomes positively alarmed when the creeping creature comes into view and turns out to be a human shape, armed with a bow and arrow and not quite six inches high! Gulliver feels about forty more of these little people crawling up his body. Absolutely astonished, he roars at the top of his lungs, frightening the little men off. He perceives, by a growing noise, that he is virtually surrounded by a small army. When he attempts to break the bonds that hold him down, the little army discharges a volley of one hundred arrows at him; painfully stung, he quickly realizes that his most prudent course is to lie still.

When order is re-established, Gulliver begins to take stock of his situation. He is rather surprised (and impressed) to see that the little people, in the few hours since they found him asleep on their shore, have made elaborate arrangements for controlling and accommodating him, although he is, after all, an enormous and terrifying giant to these little creatures. They have erected a platform near his head and, from this platform, a figure of authority delivers an address to Gulliver. Gulliver does not, of course, understand a word of the speech but he does recognize that an attempt is being made to reason with him. Gulliver takes an opportunity to indicate that he is famished and is again surprised and impressed by the elaborate preparations these little people, the Lilliputians, have made to feed him. A truly remarkable scene follows in which Gulliver eats, and drinks a bulk of food and wine which astounds the Lilliputians. He drinks two full barrels of wine (about one pint all told); he eats three loaves of bread in one gulp (each loaf is the size of a musket bullet): he takes two or three shoulders of mutton in each mouthful (a shoulder of Lilliputian mutton is smaller than the wing of an English lark). In the meantime, the Lilliputians marvel at the prodigious amounts of food their captive is able to swallow.

| Comment

This eating scene is an important example of Swift's technique in Book I. He must convince the reader of the reality of the fantastic little creatures; therefore, he describes in Lilliputian terms the amounts of food and drink consumed by Gulliver and then translates these Lilliputian quantities into human terms. Swift is very careful to establish and maintain these proportions, not only in food quantities but also in the sizes of buildings, clothes and distances. Because of the painstaking detail in which Lilliputian dimensions are related to human proportions, the reader is willing to accept the fantastic events Gulliver describes and give himself up to the narrative.

After he has eaten, Gulliver tries to make the leader of the Lilliputian band realize that he wishes to be freed. The request is denied whereupon Gulliver thinks of taking his freedom by force. He remembers, however, how painful the stings of the arrows were and decides to submit to his captors. The little creatures mount and walk all over his body investigating him and Gulliver is greatly impressed by their courage.

A messenger from the Lilliputian Emperor arrives and informs Gulliver that he is to be brought into the capital city. Swift goes into some detail describing the conveyance which the Lilliputians design for the purpose of moving the giant Gulliver into the city. As soon as Gulliver lands on the Lilliputian shore, five hundred carpenters and engineers set about building a means of transporting him into the city. They build a frame of wood raised three inches from the ground; about seven feet long and four feet wide, moving upon twenty-two wheels. It is brought up parallel to Gulliver and, with the aid of nine hundred workmen and an elaborate system of pulleys and poles, the Lilliputians succeed in placing Gulliver upon this carriage. All through this operation, he is fast asleep, drugged by a soporific that was placed in his wine.

Chained to this carriage, Gulliver is wheeled to the city by fifteen hundred of the Emperor's largest horses, each one about four and a half inches high. It is noon of the following day when the cortege reaches the city gates to be greeted by the Emperor and the entire court. The carriage stops in front of an ancient temple which had been unused for many years because it had been polluted some time back by a afoul murder perpetrated within its walls. It is decided that this temple should be the site of Gulliver's captivity. The Emperor's workmen place a length of chain on Gulliver's left leg and connect the other end of the chain to a place inside the temple. The chains are so arranged that he has considerable freedom of movement into and out of the temple and within the confines of the courtyard surrounding it. These chains are about the size of a lady's watch chain in Europe and it takes ninety-one of them to secure Gulliver.

Securely established now within the temple, Gulliver is a prime attraction to the Lilliputian people. He is viewed by the Emperor and his court and no less than one hundred thousand citizens, many of whom climb all over his body. This practice is soon terminated when a proclamation is issued forbidding any citizen, upon pain of death, to climb up on the body of the giant.

Comment

The main purpose of Chapter I is to introduce us to Gulliver and the Lilliputians. Gulliver impresses us as a rather prudent, unimaginative, ordinary sort of man. We find it somewhat amusing for example that, in the midst of so fantastic an adventure, Gulliver should have paid as much attention as he did to minute details. We are at once fascinated and bored by the detailed descriptions of what he ate, the number of creatures who served him and the manner in which he was brought into the city. He is middle aged and, up to this point in his life, has been largely concerned with preparing for and pursuing a career as a physician. It is important for Swift's purpose that Gulliver be a solid, somewhat inquisitive but by no means unusual person. For Gulliver is to be subjected, in the course of this book, to some highly unusual experiences, some of them he will understand, others he will not. Part of Swift's technique here is to create his meaning by forcing the reader to observe Gulliver's responses to these experiences; the reader will sometimes laugh at Gulliver, sometimes agree with him and sometimes pity him. It is thus through the reader's reactions to Gulliver that the meaning of Gulliver's experiences is established by Swift.

In this first chapter, Swift creates a rather favorable impression of the Lilliputians. We are impressed by their courage, their ingenuity and their apparent political prudence. Their courage is demonstrated by their willingness to come close to and walk all over and investigate the person of the giant Gulliver. Their ingenuity is demonstrated in the various devices they have prepared to handle the giant and their political prudence is seen in the "policy" they formulated to deal with the giant. They provide him with food, they supply accommodations for him and, above all, they attempt to reason with him. In this way, they make of him, as we shall see, a powerful friend and ally; whereas, had they tried to use force in controlling him, he might have destroyed them. Of course, this happy state of affairs will not continue for long; we shall see why as we become acquainted with the defects, as well as the virtues, of the Lilliputians.

CHAPTER II

From the vantage of his new living quarters, Gulliver views and is charmed by his Lilliputian surroundings. The countryside seems to him a lovely garden and the city appears "like the painted scene of a city in a theatre." However, his adjustment to life in his new environment is not without some difficulties. For example, he relates, in some detail, the problems he faced and the arrangements that were devised in accommodating his bodily functions. For two days since he had arrived on the shore of Lilliput, he had not disburdened himself because, as a giant in a land of pygmies, he had not a moment's privacy. "I was under great difficulties between urgency and shame," he tells us. "The best expedient I could think on was to creep into my house, which I accordingly did and shutting the gate after me, ... discharged my body of that uneasy load." Gulliver is quick to add that this is the only time he was ever guilty of so unclean an action. In the future, he performed "that business in open air ... and due care was taken every morning before company came that the offensive matter should be carried off in wheelbarrows." Gulliver makes a point of absolving himself of the charge of uncleanliness which, he says, had been leveled against him since his return to England.

Comment

In these few touches, we see Swift filling in his portrayal of Gulliver's character. The fact that Gulliver feels called upon to describe in detail the manner in which he attended to the necessities of nature indicates that he has a penchant for details and not much discrimination in differentiating the important from the mundane. However, in the delight he shows with his new surroundings, we see that although he is unimaginative he is a man of ready goodwill, easily pleased and prepared to enjoy his new experience.

The emperor and his court pay a visit to Gulliver who is much impressed by the appearance of these Lilliputians. The Emperor, we are told, is dressed simply but impressively "between the Asiatic and the European" fashion; the ladies and the courtiers appear to be so many "figures of gold and silver". The Emperor is handsome in the manner of a European aristocrat and is just entering middle age which, for a Lilliputian, is about twenty-nine years. The Emperor is physically awesome to his subjects because he is the tallest in his court, towering over his subjects by a height which is almost the breadth of Gulliver's fingernail.

Comment

While Gulliver relates these details and indicates that he is quite impressed, Swift is actually jibing at the Lilliputians and their Emperor. To us as readers, the Emperor's advantage in height over his subjects seems barely perceptible and, therefore, it seems ridiculous that he cuts so awesome a figure before his people. Here, Swift is, of course, using this example of Lilliputian pride to take a swipe at all monarchs and "great men" whose positions of authority have blinded them to the fact that they are still men.

The Emperor's visit ends after he and Gulliver fail to find a language which is mutually comprehensible. After the Emperor leaves, a number of the rabble who have come to gape at Gulliver amuse themselves by shooting arrows at him, but his guard seizes six of the troublemakers and delivers them over to Gulliver so that he may devise a fit punishment for them. Gulliver places them in the pocket of his coat and then takes them out, one by one, and makes a face at each one as if he were about to eat the culprit alive. He thus frightens the rude Lilliputians out of their wits but does them no harm. The Lilliputian population begins to respect Gulliver for this demonstration of his merciful nature.

In fact, Gulliver was to discover later that it was largely owing to this act of mercy on his part that the Imperial Council decided to continue to maintain and feed him; for, at this time, some of the Emperor's ministers were of the opinion that the giant should be starved to death or be shot with poisoned arrows.

Comment

While Gulliver does not seem to be unduly upset to hear that the Lilliputians are debating putting him to death, Swift subtly adds another dimension to his portrayal of the Lilliputians by telling the reader of these cruel plans and forcing the reader to contrast the mercy Gulliver has just shown with the cruelty of which the Lilliputians are capable. We see now that, in addition to being a rather prideful people, the Lilliputians are quite capable of heartless cruelty, a despicable quality, especially when we consider their rather diminutive stature. As the first book of the Travels develops, we will discover more and more evidence of the moral baseness of these little people.

When the Council is informed of Gulliver's kindness to the rabble, they decide to provide for Gulliver's support and not to put him to death. The King decrees that the village within a nine hundred yard radius of the city must deliver "every morning six beeves, forty sheep and other victuals for [Gulliver's] sustenance, together with a proportionable quantity of bread and wine and other liquors." Six hundred persons are assigned to Gulliver as his domestic servants; three hundred tailors are given the task of making the giant a suit of clothes.

The Emperor further decrees that six of the greatest scholars in the land are to teach Gulliver the Lilliputian language in which he begins to gain proficiency in a short time. With his growing command of the language, Gulliver constantly appeals to the Emperor for his freedom, begging to be unchained. The Emperor replies that if he behaves well Gulliver may expect to be given his freedom after a period of time but not before he Lumos Kelmin pesso desmar lon Emposo. This is the Lilliputian expression for "swearing a peace with the kingdom." The Emperor promises, however, that until his chains are removed Gulliver will be treated with all kindness. He asks Gulliver to cooperate in permitting himself to be searched and Gulliver willingly assents. There follows a most amusing account of the search through Gulliver's pockets. The Lilliputians are mystified by the strange objects in the pockets of Quinbus Flestrin, the man mountain, as they call Gulliver. Here, for example, is their response to his watch: "Out of the right fob hung a great silver chain with a wonderful kind of engine at the bottom. We directed him to draw out whatever was at the end of that chain, which appeared to be a globe, half silver and half of some transparent metal: for on the transparent side we saw certain strange figures circularly drawn and, thought we could touch them, until we found our fingers stopped with that lucid substance. He put this engine to our ears, which made an incessant noise like that of a water-mill. And we conjectured it is either some unknown animal or the god that he worships. But we are more inclined to the latter opinion because he assured us ... that he seldom did anything without consulting it."

After his pockets are searched, Gulliver delivers over to the Lilliputians his sword and his pistols but not before he frightens them nearly to death by demonstrating the firing of the guns. Chapter II ends with the prudent Gulliver informing us that he did not permit the searchers to discover his spectacles since, "I apprehended that they might be lost or spoiled if I ventured them out of my possession."

Comment

The reader should begin to be aware of the use Swift makes of the device of portraying the Lilliputians as physical pygmies. From one point of view, of course, their achievements are all the more remarkable to us in the light of their tiny stature but, when we come to consider their moral qualities, we will see that they are quite capable of "man size" vices. Their diminutive stature in no way diminishes their vices. Quite the contrary, it is their pygmy stature which makes all the more ironic and reprehensible the fact that they can be prideful, vicious and cruel. However, at this point in the book, Swift merely hints at these aspects of Lilliputian character. As Chapter II ends, both the reader and Gulliver are rather charmed by the little creatures but the reader, thanks to Swift, is growing somewhat suspicious of them.

CHAPTER III

Gulliver soon becomes a favorite of the Emperor and the Lilliputian people who no longer fear him in any way. He creates diversions for them by permitting them to dance in his hands and allowing the children to play hide and seek in his hair. He makes considerable progress in learning the language and is allowed to view some of the favorite pastimes of the Lilliputian court.

One of these court diversions is rope dancing. It is practiced only by those who hope to achieve high positions in the service of the Emperor. The candidates for a vacant office assemble before the Emperor and the court and entertain them by a dance on a rope which is held six inches above the floor. Standing on the rope, the candidate must jump in the air and land with his two feet on the rope. Whoever jumps highest without falling off the rope wins the office. On frequent occasions, those who have in the past won high offices in this manner are called upon to perform the rope dance again to show that they have not lost their skill. Gulliver tells us that the treasurer of the realm, Flimnap, is the nation's most accomplished rope dancer while Reldresal, the principal secretary for private affairs (and later Gulliver's friend) is a close second to Flimnap. Gulliver remarks that, under this system, the candidate for great employments and high favor is not necessarily distinguished by noble birth or liberal education. As we shall see, neither is he necessarily distinguished by merit.

Another favorite court diversion involves an unusual "trial of dexterity." The candidates here compete for the Emperor's favor by leaping over or creeping under a stick which the Emperor raises and lowers at his will. The best leaper and creeper is rewarded by receiving a blue silken thread, six inches long; the two runners-up are awarded red and green threads respectively. Gulliver tells us that almost all of the important court figures are adorned with these signs of the Emperor's favor.

| Comment

While Gulliver is apparently charmed by these popular Lilliputian customs, we can perceive (between the lines) the satiric intention of Swift. He is, of course, using the rope dancing and leaping and creeping as devices to portray the Lilliputian government as corrupt; government office is not the reward for personal merit but rather the payoff for pleasing the Emperor and his minister. To us, the readers, the "tricks" performed before the Emperor seem demeaning; thus, the "performers" are men who are willing to give up their dignity in return for political reward. In fact, the willingness to debase oneself before the Emperor, to do "tricks" for him, so to speak, is a necessary condition for high office. We are thus made to see that, at bottom, Lilliputian political life is corrupt. Swift, of course, is writing here about English political life under his enemies, the Whigs. Most commentators agree that Flimnap, the proficient rope dancer, represents Sir Robert Walpole, the Whig Prime Minister who was detested by Swift and who is notorious for basing his political strategy upon bribery and favoritism.

Gulliver tells us of an entertainment he devises which particularly pleases the Emperor. He constructs a little military drill field by stretching his handkerchief over a number of small, upright sticks. The Emperor is pleased to see a company of his cavalry lifted on to the tautly drawn handkerchief upon which they perform maneuvers. Luckily for Gulliver, no serious accidents occur during these exercises but, on one occasion, a fiery horse paws a hole in the handkerchief: his leg slips through the hole and the rider is thrown but not hurt. After this incident, Gulliver puts an end to this diversion.

Another way in which Gulliver satisfies the Emperor's fondness for pageantry is to stand with his legs spread apart while the Emperor's horse soldiers pass through his legs in review. The cavalrymen cannot help glancing upwards and snickering at the poor condition of Gulliver's breeches and the impressive size of his genitalia but the Emperor forbids such snickering on the pain of death. At this point in the narrative,

Gulliver considers it important to tell us in some detail of the manner in which the Lilliputians found his hat lying on the seashore, were amazed by it, and dragged it into the city, so mauling it that it could never be worn again.

Comment

In the above mentioned games and in the **episode** of Gulliver's hat, Swift reminds us again of the disparity in size between Gulliver and the Lilliputians. It is important that we do not overlook the fact that the Lilliputians are laughably tiny. Swift will capitalize on their physical insignificance in order to make his satiric point later on in this chapter.

Gulliver's paramount desire continues to be his liberty. He finds that the Emperor's cabinet is willing to grant it to him. However, one of the most influential men in the kingdom, the Admiral of the realm, one Skyresh Bolgolam, has, for no reason whatsoever, chosen to consider Gulliver his enemy. Bolgolam strongly opposes granting the giant his liberty. Nevertheless, the cabinet is overwhelmingly in favor of unchaining Gulliver and Bolgolam is persuaded to comply with this policy. However, to assuage his pride, Bolgolam is given the authority to draw up the terms under which Gulliver it to be set free. Bolgolam stipulates nine conditions: first, Gulliver must not depart from Lilliput without official permission: second, Gulliver must not enter the great city without official permission and at least two hours warning; third, Gulliver must walk on the high roads, and not walk or lie down in meadows or farms; fourth, when Gulliver walks on the roads, he must take great care not to trample the Lilliputian people or their horses, nor is he allowed to take any Lilliputian into his hands unless the citizen so consents; fifth, Gulliver must put himself at the disposal of the Emperor as a messenger for a period of six days in every moon; sixth, Gulliver must fight for the Lilliputians in their war against their enemies, the Blefuscudians; seventh, in his leisure time Gulliver shall aid the Lilliputian workmen in the lifting of heavy stones for construction work; eighth, Gulliver must, in two months time, deliver to the Emperor "an exact survey of the circumference of our dominions, by a computation of his own paces round the coast"; ninth and last, on the condition of his swearing to observe the above eight articles, Gulliver shall have a daily allowance of meat and drink sufficient for the support of one thousand, seven hundred and twenty-eight Lilliputians.

Gulliver readily assents to these conditions although he recognizes that some of them proceeded from the malice of Bolgolam; one does not, after all, impose official obligations on another unless he distrusts that person's honesty and doubts that he will act with honor. (As we shall see, it will be Gulliver who will have occasion to complain about Lilliputian honor. They, and not he, will behave deceitfully.) At any rate, as Chapter III ends, Gulliver's chains are removed.

Comment

This is an important chapter. In it, Swift continues his portrayal of Gulliver as good natured and somewhat naive but he subtly intensifies his attack on the Lilliputians. It is an attack based upon their political institutions and their pride. The tiny creatures are shown to live under a corrupt and autocratic monarch and, worse, the court surrounding the King is shown to be composed of men who are quite willing to let themselves be corrupted. In addition, Swift draws a connection between the corruption of the Lilliputian government and the vice of pride which so taints these tiny creatures. That they are prideful is obvious when we consider (1) their presumption in dictating terms to the giant Gulliver who could, if he wished, stamp them out with a few kicks and (2) the impudence of Bolgolam who presumes to conceive of the Man Mountain (Gulliver) as a personal enemy and therefore as at least an equal of Bolgolam. Swift seems to be saying that a corrupt government is the result of evil men and the source of all evil in man is pride, or one's failure to recognize what one is. The Lilliputians do not seem to realize how weak they are in relation to the giant they presume to control. The sin of pride is all the more laughable and despicable in these creatures when we consider their tiny stature. Swift's satiric genius is seen in his device of portraying the fault of pride in creatures whose physical size, from our (and Gulliver's) point of view, makes them laughably insignificant. Gulliver, though he is fascinated by the physical disparity between himself and his hosts, is unaware, at this point, of the moral disparity between them.

CHAPTER IV

Upon receiving his liberty, Gulliver is granted permission to see the great Lilliputian metropolis, Mildendo. The Emperor warns him not to harm the inhabitants who crowd their rooftops to watch the Man Mountain walk through their streets. Mildendo is encompassed by a wall two and one half feet high and eleven inches broad. (To get an idea of what these dimensions are, in human terms, multiply the dimensions by twelve.) It is clear that this wall is an impressive structure. Gulliver steps over the wall and walks very carefully through the streets. The city, he discovers, is in the shape of a perfect square; five hundred feet on each side. Two great streets, five feet wide, run diagonally across the city, dividing it into four quarters. The lanes and alleys of Mildendo are from twelve to eighteen inches wide. The city is capable of holding a population of one half million. At the center of the city, where the two great streets intersect, is the Emperor's Palace, enclosed by a wall two feet high. Since the buildings of the palace are about five feet high.

Gulliver cannot step over them without damaging them. He therefore builds two stools which he uses as ladders to permit him to step over the buildings and thus into the inner court of the palace from which he can look into the royal apartments. The Empress smiles graciously from her window and gives Gulliver her hand to kiss. Gulliver is mightily impressed by the splendor of these royal lodgings. He cuts short his description of them, however, by telling the reader that he has prepared a detailed account of Lilliputian life in another volume almost ready for the press.

Comment

Swift is adding to his portrayal of the Lilliputians here, calling attention to their ingenuity (here seen in their impressive feats of city planning and architecture). Technological competence is thus seen to be no guarantee of moral virtue. Gulliver, we see, is still charmed and impressed by the accomplishments of his diminutive hosts and he seems to relish the opportunity of describing their city in minute detail.

About two weeks after Gulliver is set free, he is paid a visit by Reldresal, the principal Secretary of Private Affairs. Sent by the Emperor, Reldresal has come to inform Gulliver of some features of Lilliputian history and current problems. All is not well in the Lilliputian land and the nation is beset with two great difficulties, violent political division at home and the danger of invasion by a powerful enemy from abroad.

The violent political controversy in Lilliput is between two major factions: the Tramecksans and the Slamecksans, respectively known as the "high heels" and the "low heels" by which they distinguish themselves in their dress. The Emperor is a low heel and it is his intention to exclude the high heels from all government office. The high heels exceed the low heels in numbers but the low heels have all the political power in the land. The two parties hate each other with a vengeance and the situation is even more troubled because of the Emperor's son (the heir to the crown) who, unlike his father, leans toward the high heels. The Prince's unclear position is seen in his shoes; one of which has a heel slightly higher than that on the other shoe, causing him to walk with a hobble.

Comment

The political feuding in Lilliput refers, of course, to the contemporary political divisions in Swift's England. We may take the High Heels to represent the Tories who were out of favor with George I, while the English Whigs are represented by the Low Heels. Swift, who was a Tory, nevertheless regarded violent political controversy as a sign of the moral decadence of a nation. Thus, we now see that there is something rotten at the heart of Lilliputian (and English) society and this rottenness is signified by the violent political dissension which tears at the strength of the nation. The device of presenting political differences in terms of the height of one's heels serves, of course, to show how ridiculous such controversy is when seen in the perspective of common sense.

In addition to the evil of internal division, Reldresal informs Gulliver of yet another great problem facing the Lilliputians: the threat of invasion from Blefuscu, the great rival power. Lilliput and Blefuscu have been at war for some thirty-six moons and this war is related to yet another controversy in Lilliput, a religious one. The present Emperor's grandfather, having cut his hand one morning as he was opening his egg on the larger end (as was the religious custom) issued a decree to his subjects making it mandatory for them to break their eggs on the smaller end. This new dogma immediately aroused violent resentment and, in the course of years, caused six rebellions. Eleven thousand people preferred to lose their lives rather than break their eggs in the new way. This religious strife between the Big-Endians and the Little-Endians (as the two groups came to be called) was frequently exploited by the Emperor of Blefuscu for political purposes: the Big-Endians appealed to him for support and, when they were defeated, fled to Blefuscu as Lilliputian exiles. Aided by the Emperor of Blefuscu, the Big-Endians are currently planning a massive invasion of Lilliput, the result of which can only benefit Blefuscu. Thus, the Emperor of Lilliput has sent Reldresal to Gulliver in order to request Gulliver's aid in the coming battle. Gulliver replies that he will give whatever help he can to the Emperor against his foreign foes but will not interfere in purely internal matters.

Comment

Many references to English political, religious and diplomatic history are involved in this matter of the egg-breaking controversy. England was torn by religious strife throughout the seventeenth century between the various factions of Protestant belief. Beyond this, there existed a deep-seated fear and distrust of Catholicism. The dispute between the Big-Endians and Little-Endians reflects these two aspects of religious controversy in England but particularly the second. This latter involved England's relations with the Catholic kingdom of France which was always suspected of fomenting plots to establish a Catholic monarch on the English throne and with which England had been at war early in the 18th century (the War of the Spanish Succession). Thus, we may interpret the Empire of Blefuscu to stand for France. Swift, of course, is doing more than writing political allegory here. He is attacking the strife born of religious dispute and is mocking religious dispute itself and showing it to involve heated passions over apparently ridiculous issues, as ridiculous as the question of which end of an egg to break in order to eat it.

CHAPTER V

Gulliver formulates a plan for seizing the entire Blefuscudian fleet. Blefuscu lies north-north-east of Lilliput, separated by about eight hundred yards of water from her enemy. After determining that the water is only seventy glumgluffs deep at its deepest (about six feet) Gulliver calls for a great quantity of cable and iron bars (the cable was the thickness of packthread, the bars as big as knitting needles) from which he fashions hooks and lines to be used in his plan. Having counted fifty warships in the enemy's fleet, Gulliver connects fifty hooks to fifty cables and crosses the channel, half wading and half swimming. This takes him half an hour.

The Blefuscudian sailors are alarmed when they see him; they abandon their ships and swim to shore. Gulliver then begins to connect a cable to each of the fifty ships and then ties all fifty cables together at their ends. The Blefuscudians, meanwhile, are discharging thousands of arrows at Gulliver and he, in fear of having his eyes damaged, puts on his spectacles. With a cable connected to each Blefuscudian ship, Gulliver begins to draw the warships along to Lilliput but the ships do not budge. He finds it necessary to cut their anchors; in the process, he is hit with two hundred arrows but he succeeds in drawing off the entire Blefuscudian fleet. The Blefuscudians cry in grief and despair as they see their warships being led away.

Gulliver approaches the Lilliputian shore shouting, "Long live the most puissant Emperor of Lilliput!" The Emperor, overjoyed at Gulliver's success, bestows upon the Man Mountain the highest Lilliputian honor - the title of Nardac.

However, the Lilliputian Emperor, not satisfied with having captured all the warships of his enemy, asks Gulliver to make similar plans for the capture of every Blefuscudian ship. Gulliver perceives that the Emperor would be pleased to use him in order to destroy completely the Blefuscudian empire and to reduce it to a Lilliputian colony and, in the process, destroy the Big-Endian exiles. In other words, the Emperor wishes to become the ruler of what to him seems to be the entire world. Gulliver is horrified at the thought and refuses to help the Emperor in this project. Gulliver's refusal is supported by several of the Emperor's wisest ministers but it is also the cause of the Emperor's growing coolness towards Gulliver.

Comment

Gulliver's capture of the Blefuscudian fleet has been interpreted to represent the action of the Tory leaders in arranging an end to the war between England and France (War of the Spanish Succession). More importantly, the whole **episode**, including the Emperor's request that Gulliver seize all the Blefuscudian ships, is a further development of the attack of the Lilliputians: Swift here develops another aspect of their basic sin of pride.

We now see that pride results in the desire for unbridled power and is thus the cause of tyranny. The good-natured Gulliver, not beset with pride, is horrified at the Emperor's request.

About three weeks after Gulliver destroys their navy, the Blefuscudians send a delegation to Lilliput to negotiate a peace treaty which is concluded with terms quite favorable to the Lilliputians. The Blefuscudians thank Gulliver for refusing to reduce them to slavery and they invite him to visit their Emperor. He accepts the invitation but notices that the Lilliputian emperor consents only grudgingly to Gulliver's visiting Blefuscu. This is because a group of ministers (including Flimnap and Bolgolam), aware of the Emperor's anger at the Man Mountain for his refusal utterly to subdue the Blefuscudians, attempt to capitalize upon that anger and create further division between the Emperor and Gulliver. They, therefore, tell the Emperor that Gulliver's wish to visit Blefuscu is a sign that the giant is angry at the Lilliputian Emperor. This is untrue but it serves to make the Emperor even more cool towards Gulliver who remarks that "this was the first time I began to conceive some imperfect idea of courts and ministers."

Comment

This is an important moment in the book because it is the first indication of Gulliver's growing awareness of the corrupt intriguing which lies at the heart of Lilliputian political life. Gulliver begins to be aware that honesty and merit are doomed in this environment. Notice that it was his capturing the enemy fleet (a great service to the state) that actually got him into trouble because it engendered jealousy in those surrounding the Emperor. Because of their own pride, Flimnap and Bolgolam would rather get rid of Gulliver than recognize him as a powerful friend to their nation. Thus, we see how pride can stand in the way of true patriotism.

Gulliver makes some observations about the differences between the Lilliputian and Blefuscudian languages. He tells us that these are quite distinct but that there are a great number in each kingdom who can converse in both tongues, particularly among the richer gentry whose custom it is to travel in the other country as a means of enhancing their education. (Obviously, this parallels the relationship between England and France. It was a common custom for rich, young Englishmen to tour France.)

Gulliver has a strange adventure some weeks after the preceding events. He is awakened one clear night and asked to help put out a fire in the Empress's apartment. He rushes to the palace and sees that the fire is too violent to be controlled by the Lilliputian bucket brigade whose buckets are thimble-sized. Having consumed a great deal of wine earlier in the evening and, not having discharged any of it yet, Gulliver was able to unleash a prodigious amount of urine on the fire. In three minutes, he puts out the fire. The Empress, however, being rather shortsighted, is more annoyed at the manner in which the fire was quenched than pleased that the palace was saved. Because of her anger, Gulliver is never pardoned officially for urinating on the palace: a deed punishable by death according to the laws of Lilliput. The angry Empress never again lives in that part of the palace saved by Gulliver's ingenuity. Moreover, this incident is later used by Flimnap and Bolgolam to deepen the Queen's growing antagonism towards Gulliver. It is thus the beginning of Gulliver's troubles in Lilliput. It is generally agreed that, allegorically, Gulliver's putting out the palace fire represents the signing of the Treaty of Utrecht which put an end to the War of the Spanish Succession-a war in which England was inconveniently embroiled. The Tories arranged for the peace, but were to meet much criticism on that score from the Whigs, just as Gulliver does from Bolgolam and Flimnap for putting out the fire.

CHAPTER VI

Gulliver devotes the largest part of this section of his adventures in Lilliput to a description and discussion of some of the more fascinating aspects of Lilliputian society. He is still charmed by the fact that the Lilliputians and their environment are perfect copies in miniature of human beings and human surroundings; the people are six inches tall and everything else is in proportion to them. A sheep stands an inch and a half high; geese are as large as our sparrows; larks are the size of common houseflies; and the largest trees are but seven feet tall.

After mentioning these physical details, Gulliver proceeds to discuss several aspects of Lilliputian customs, laws and history. He notes that they have a long and flourishing tradition of scholarship but he is most interested in their peculiar manner of writing "aslant from one corner of the paper to the other, like ladies in England." They have the strange custom of burying their dead upside down because they believe that, on Judgment Day, the world will turn upside down and thus the dead will be right side up on the occasion of their resurrection. The learned Lilliputians scoff at this idea, however.

Most unusual are the laws of the little people. If an accused man is found innocent, his accuser is immediately put to death. Fraud is thought to be a more serious crime than theft because all commercial and social relationships are endangered by fraud whereas the consequences of theft are not generally very serious. Most remarkable, however, is the fact that Lilliputian law is based not only upon punishment of the guilty but, also, upon reward for the virtuous. Any man who shows that he has obeyed the law for seventy-three moons is awarded a sum of money and the title of Snilpall (which means Legal).

Gulliver points out that the Lilliputians, in selecting people for important government positions, are more concerned that the officeholders be men of good morals than men of high ability. Government, they feel, is no difficult art; if one can direct his own life according to truth, justice, temperance, etc., then he can direct a nation. In fact, men of high ability can be a danger to their nation: a man of great intelligence may use his gifts to evil ends. (This is an important idea to Swift who would have had serious reservations about the kind of government by experts we have become dependent upon today.) Furthermore, since the Lilliputian Emperor, like the European king, believes he derives his authority from God, no man may hold a public office who does not believe in Divine Providence.

Gulliver now takes a moment to emphasize that these rather admirable beliefs, customs and laws which he has just described are not actually observed by the present Lilliputians. Rather, these are the original institutions which have been, in the course of Lilliputian history, corrupted until a situation exists in which a man wins offices and rewards not for his merits but, instead, for his rope-dancing (as we have seen in Chapter III). Gulliver attributes this decline in Lilliputian political morality to the degenerate nature of man and to the increase of internal division in the nation ("party and faction" in Swift's own terms).

Comment

This is an important moment in the book. For one thing, in his short account of Lilliputian society, Swift really is attacking his contemporary England. Like Lilliput, England too once had good institutions and just and honest governors; but, like Lilliput, England has declined. It is a country torn apart by the warring factions of ambitious politicians; a country of frauds and informers: a country where it is unsafe to be good. Swift makes this attack indirectly, leaving it to us to infer the existence of those evils by telling us of the disappearance of their corresponding virtues. In addition, if we consider Gulliver himself at this point, we can see the further growth of his disillusionment with the Lilliputians. He expresses his awareness of the great discrepancy between their ideals and their actual way of life.

Gulliver is fascinated by the beliefs the Lilliputians have concerning relations between parents and children. The Lilliputians do not believe that children owe any gratitude to their parents for being brought into the world nor for education which is supplied by the state. The children attend school from the ages of four to twelve; the length of one's education depends upon one's social class. There are different schools for children of different social classes. The children live at school and see their parents only twice a year. One gathers that relations between parents and children are not especially affectionate.

In order to clothe and feed their giant guest, the Lilliputians employ three hundred tailors, three hundred cooks and one hundred-twenty waiters. This is a great expense to the nation; Gulliver's enemy, Flimnap, estimating the cost at a million and a half sprugs (Lilliputian currency) tries to convince the

Emperor to put an end to the expense by getting rid of Gulliver. The Emperor, however, does not heed Flimnap's advice at this time when several other enemies of Gulliver are spreading rumors that there is a scandalous attachment between the giant and Flimnap's wife. Gulliver vehemently denies the accusation proclaiming that he never entertained any ladies unless they were accompanied by their friends. Flimnap eventually admits that he was wrong about his wife but the matter serves only to alienate him further from Gulliver.

Comment

This last matter concerning Gulliver's supposedly illicit affair with Flimnap's wife is a further and slyly humorous expose of the preposterous pride of the little people; they are blind to their limitations. A Lilliputian is, after all, only six inches tall, Gulliver is six feet. A love affair is obviously physically impossible. The student should note that this incident is also a satiric slap at Walpole, who is represented by Flimnap.

CHAPTER VII

Gulliver has not yet made his visit to the king of Blefuscu but, before this chapter ends, he will make that visit ... never again to return to Lilliput for (without his realizing it) during the last two months of his nine month stay in Lilliput, his enemies Flimnap and Bolgolam have been developing their plot against him and have succeeded in winning the Emperor to their side. The Emperor, it will be remembered, has harbored a grudge against Gulliver even since the Man Mountain refused to subdue completely the Blefuscudians.

Just before Gulliver departs for his visit to Blefuscu, he is paid an unexpected visit one night by a person of considerable importance in the court of the Lilliputian Emperor. This person, whose name Gulliver never divulges, informs the Giant of the plot against him. Bolgolam, the Admiral (who has been jealous of Gulliver ever since the giant captured the Blefuscudian fleet), Flimnap, the treasurer, and three other high Lilliputian officials have drawn up an indictment against Gulliver charging him with treason and other capital crimes. There were four counts to the indictment: the first charged Gulliver with treason for urinating on the palace in order to put out the fire; the second condemned him for refusing to reduce the Blefuscudians to slavery; the third count charges Gulliver with being unnecessarily decent and courteous to the Blefuscudian ambassadors who came to negotiate a peace treaty; the fourth article maintains that Gulliver intends to visit Blefuscu without written permission from the Lilliputian Emperor and with the purpose of aiding and comforting the Blefuscudian Emperor.

The plotters have some difficulty in agreeing upon the punishment which is to be meted out to Gulliver for his supposed crimes. Bolgolam and Flimnap demand that he be put to a cruel death by being burned alive in his house, shot with poisoned arrows, and covered with a poisonous liquid which would make him tear his flesh. Reldresal, Gulliver's friend, urges mercy, suggesting that his eyes be put out but that his life be spared. When Flimnap and Bolgolam strenuously object to this, a compromise is arrived at according to which Gulliver is to be blinded and slowly starved to death over a period of months. It is decided that the blinding will be accomplished by twenty of the Emperor's surgeons who will discharge sharp arrows into the giant's eyes while he humbly and gratefully lies on the ground. This punishment is decided upon in the name of mercy.

Comment

The moral blindness of the Lilliputians is conveyed here by means of a bitter joke: so blinded are they by their pride that they apparently do not realize how ridiculous it is for such tiny creatures to presume to condemn and punish a giant who could, were he as rotten as they, destroy them with a stamp of his foot. Swift emphasizes the physical details of their plans to blind Gulliver in order to convey to us the cruelty of which these odious little creatures are capable. We are further horrified at the fact that they sincerely believe that they are being merciful in deciding to blind Gulliver and starve him gradually instead of killing him immediately.

Upon hearing of the evil plans that are being made, Gulliver admits that he cannot detect any mercy in them, try as he may. For a short while, he is unsure as to a course of action: should he defend himself and declare his innocence of the charges or should he flee? His decision is interesting; he decides not to defend himself because, although he realizes that he could easily destroy the Lilliputians, he does not want to do so. He reasons that the Lilliputians have treated him with kindness at first and, therefore, malicious as they may be now, it would be ungrateful of him to cause them any grief.

Comment

Swift is drawing a dramatic contrast between the good-natured and highly moral behavior of the mighty Man Mountain and the cruel ingratitude of his diminutive enemies. Gulliver's behavior thus represents that of the ordinary, decent human being while the Lilliputians display a kind of behavior of which man is capable at his worst. Notice the **irony**: Gulliver (who has all the strength) has all the kindness; the Lilliputians (physically insignificant) are as cruel "as giants."

Resolving to leave Lilliput, Gulliver sends a note to Reldresal informing him of his intention and, without waiting for an answer, sets out for Blefescu towing behind him a Lilliputian ship within which he has placed his clothes so that he may swim freely. In a short while, he arrives in Blefescu where he is greeted courteously and without fear.

CHAPTER VIII

Three days after coming to Blefescu, Gulliver, in exploring the north-east coast of the island, spies an overturned, human-sized row boat several hundred yards offshore. Gulliver immediately begins to think of the boat as a means of escape to England and, with the aid of twenty of the largest Blefuscudian vessels and three thousands of her seamen, he succeeds in landing the boat on the beach. He then succeeds in turning the boat on its bottom whereupon he discovers that it will need minor repairs. He fashions a pair of crude paddles and manages to row the boat to the royal port of Blefescu where he may do the necessary work on it in order to prepare it for his voyage away from Blefuscu.

Meanwhile, the Lilliputian Emperor, not realizing that Gulliver is aware of the plot against him, is undisturbed at first by Gulliver's visit to Blefuscu; but, as days pass without any indication that the giant will return to Lilliput, the Emperor sends an ambassador to Blefuscu with a copy of the indictment against Gulliver who is warned that unless he returns within two hours to Lilliput he will be deprived of his title of Nardac and will be declared a traitor. Furthermore, the king of Blefescu is ordered to bind Gulliver hand and foot and send him back to

Lilliput. After carefully considering this Lilliputian request, the king of Blefescu courteously but firmly refuses to have anything to do with sending Gulliver back to Lilliput. The Blefuscudian monarch explains that, whereas Gulliver had done him great injury in depriving him of his fleet, nevertheless he had great obligations to the Man Mountain who had refused to reduce his kingdom to a Lilliputian colony. Furthermore, it would be clearly impossible to capture and bind the giant Gulliver. The Lilliputian Emperor, however, is informed of Gulliver's discovery of a boat and of his preparations for departure: in a few weeks "both empires would be freed from so insupportable an incumbrance."

This is what the Blefescudian king tells the Lilliputian Emperor. In strictest secrecy, however, he offers Gulliver his protection against the Lilliputians if Gulliver will consent to remain in Blefescu in the service of the king. Gulliver believes that the king is sincere in his offer but, nevertheless, the giant courteously refuses the offer; his Lilliputian experience has taught him "never more to put any confidence in princes or ministers where I could possibly avoid it."

Comment

The reader should note that an important change has taken place in Gulliver since the beginning of his Lilliputian adventure. He has lost his naivete and, along with it, much of the natural goodwill and good nature that made him respond so affectionately at first to the little creatures. Thus, the first step in his education into the reality of human nature ends with disillusionment at the discovery of the meanness of which men are capable when driven by pride. He is particularly skeptical now of the behavior of "princes and ministers"; that is, he is disillusioned at the very process of government; seeing it as a hotbed of corruption, intrigue and uncontrolled ambition.

Gulliver continues to prepare for departure. Five hundred Blefuscudian workmen are employed in making two sails for his boat. Gulliver makes the necessary ropes and cables for it by twisting together as many as thirty of the thickest Blefuscudian cables. The tallow of three hundred cows serves as weatherproofing for the little boat and a great stone is its anchor. Gulliver cuts down some of the largest timber for his oars and masts.

In about a month, he is ready to depart. At the leave-taking ceremony, Gulliver lies down on his side in order to kiss the hands of the king, the queen and the princes. The king presents Gulliver with fifty purses each holding two hundred sprugs; in addition, the king gives him a gift of the royal picture. Gulliver stocks his boat with the carcasses of one hundred oxen, three hundred sheep, and a large amount of prepared meat provided by four hundred cooks. He also brings along six cows and two bulls with an equal number of ewes and rams. It is his intention to bring these animals back to England alive in order to breed them. The Emperor refuses to permit him to take along any Blefuscudian citizens.

Gulliver departs from Blefuscu on September 24, 1701, at six in the morning. Four hours later, he comes upon a small island where he stops and sleeps. The next morning, he sets out to sea once again and in a short time spots a sail in the distance. He is able to catch up with the ship early the following evening and is taken aboard. He is delighted to discover that he has happened upon an English ship returning to England from Japan. John Biddle is the captain and, on board, is one Peter Williams, an old friend of Gulliver's. Williams is sure that Gulliver is raving mad when Gulliver relates to him his adventures among the tiny folk of Lilliput and Blefuscu. He is convinced, however, of the amazing truth of Gulliver's story when he is shown the tiny animals, the gold sprugs and the portrait of the Blefuscudian king. One of these tiny sheep is eaten by a rat during the course of the voyage but the rest arrive safely in England with Gulliver.

Gulliver reaches England on April 13th, 1702. He makes a good deal of money by showing the tiny animals to the public and sells them for six hundred pounds.

In addition to the money he makes by selling the Blefuscudian cattle, Gulliver discovers that he has come into a small inheritance from his Uncle John. Thus, in about two months (when Gulliver again is moved by an urge to travel), he is able to leave his wife and family well supplied with money. He places fifteen hundred pounds with his wife. He takes leave of her, his son Johnny and his daughter Betty, and goes aboard the ship Adventure, commanded by John Nicholas and bound for Surat. What happens to him on this voyage is the subject of the second part of his Travels.

Comment

The reader will notice that, in the account of Gulliver's return home and subsequent departure, Swift burdens the reader with countless apparently insignificant little details. Swift's purpose, after all, is to make a fantastic story believable, to fool the reader, so to speak. This is accomplished by including so many matter-of-fact details in the narrative that, when the reader is finished with this first book, his overall impression is that he has been reading a factual account of an unusual, but by no means unbelievable journey.

ANALYSIS OF PART ONE OF GULLIVER'S TRAVELS

Gulliver's Travels should be read as an investigation into the nature of man ... his frailties, his capabilities and, considering these, the manner of life proper for him. Throughout the book, we find that Swift constantly emphasizes the evil of human pride as the greatest defect in human nature. Again and again, he shows us the dangerous consequences of our refusal to recognize our limitations as human beings. He has chosen, in this first part of the *Travels*, to take a simple, good natured man, Gulliver, who has not thought much about life and to place this fellow into a situation in which he becomes the victim of the rampant pride of an odious race of tiny creatures-creatures who behave as if they were the lords and masters of the universe, apparently unaware of how ridiculous their pretensions are in relation to their size. The Lilliputians, of course, are merely representatives of the human race in general, for we, too, if we consider how small we are in relation to the universe, are ludicrous if we take ourselves and our pretensions too seriously. In the course of his adventures among these little people, Gulliver comes to understand that pride is the basic human sin, the cause of all other evils as, for example, it is the cause of political corruption in Lilliput and Gulliver, once full of simple, uncritical good nature, escapes from Lilliput considerably disillusioned about the goodness of man. This is only the beginning, however, of his "education." In the sections to follow, we will watch him undergo the shattering experience of discovering that he too shares in the general, corrupt, and prideful human condition.

GULLIVER'S TRAVELS

TEXTUAL ANALYSIS

BOOK II

INTRODUCTORY NOTE

In dealing with Book II of the *Travels*, the readers must grasp the implications of Swift's technique of placing Gulliver amidst a nation of giants. What is the meaning of this shift in physical perspective? Is Swift merely demonstrating his ingenuity or is he suggesting, along with the shift in physical perspective, a corresponding shift in moral perspective?

The reader will remember that, throughout Book I, we share with Gulliver a rather condescending view of the Lilliputians; they are morally, as well as physically, inferior to us. When Book I ends, we have a sense of our own benevolent good nature as opposed to the odious pride and cruelty of the tiny Lilliputians but, in Book II, Swift has a cruel surprise in store for us. We, along with Gulliver, are forced to see ourselves in Brobdingnagian terms; in other words, we and Gulliver are to the giants of Brobdingnag as the pygmies of Lilliput were to us. Under the pressure of Brobdingnagian scrutiny, we will find ourselves identifying with Gulliver as he ridiculously attempts to assert himself and his worth against the cool disdain of the giants. In the process, Swift forces us to see that Gulliver is guilty of the same sins as were the Lilliputians; and the cruelest joke is that Swift arranges our sympathies in such a way that (in identifying with Gulliver) we condemn ourselves for we, too, are thus seen to be Lilliputians at heart.

CHAPTER I

So restless is he with home life that Gulliver sets out on another voyage scarcely two months after his return from Lilliput. On June 20, 1702, he boards the ship Adventure, commanded by Captain John Nicholas, bound for Surat. The ship arrives at the Cape of Good Hope and puts in for the winter in order to repair a leak in its hull. The following March they set sail and run into no trouble until the middle of April when, upon arriving at the Straits of Madagascar, the ship runs into a violent storm which lasts for some twenty days. After the storm subsides, the Captain maintains the last course of the ship but the storm has blown the ship so far off course that no one on board has any idea of the ship's true position.

On June 16, land is sighted; the next day, the ship anchors near the land and sends a search party ashore to explore the country. Gulliver is among this party: they attempt to find freshwater but have no success. Gulliver separates himself from the rest of the party and explores the country for about a mile inland. Finding nothing to interest him, he returns to the shore only to discover that the rest of the men, pursued by a gigantic human creature, are rowing frantically toward the ship. Gulliver does not wait to witness the results of the chase although he later discovers that the men reached the ship safely. He turns and runs back into the country he has just explored and finds a road along which a barley field is planted. Suddenly, he spies the approach of one of the farmworkers, a prodigious giant as tall as a church steeple, whose every stride is some thirty yards long. Gulliver dashes into the barley field and tries to hide himself among the plants which are forty feet high. The giant calls to another group of workers in a voice like thunder and he is joined by seven other giants with harvesting tools. Gulliver is petrified at the sight of these enormous men with their enormous cutting tools and he runs to a distant part of the barley field but is stymied by the thick growth. As he hears the giants slowly approach him, he feels that his end has come and he bemoans his fate, berating himself for leaving his home. Just as he is about to be stepped on by one of the giants, Gulliver screams as loudly as he can. The giant, surprised at the sounds, looks all around him and finally notices Gulliver. The giant very cautiously approaches him, thinking Gulliver to be some strange, dangerous little animal. The harvester picks Gulliver up and holds him in his hands, some sixty feet off the ground. Gulliver makes a begging motion with his hands trying to impress the giant that he is not some dangerous insect and hoping that the giant will not dash him to the ground. Evidently, the giant understands and he brings Gulliver (in the pocket of his jacket) to his master who is apparently the owner of the farm.

Gulliver doffs his hat, bows, falls on his knees, and presents his purse with its gold coins to the giant farmer. He does all of this in order to try to convince the giants that he is a man, not some strange beast. Evidently, he has some success in this because the farmer speaks to him and decides to bring him home to show him to his wife. Upon seeing Gulliver, the farmer's wife screams "as women in England do at the sight of a toad or a spider." In a short time, however, the lady of the house grows very fond of her tiny guest.

Comment

Gulliver appears to the Brobdingnagians the way the Lilliputians appeared to him. These giant humans are amazed at the little man but they react to him at first as if he were a dangerous little animal like a weasel. Gulliver is thus made to feel something less than human and we, the readers, are trapped into identifying with and pitying him. At this point in the narrative, however, Gulliver is too fearful for his survival to comprehend fully the insults to his pride that the giants unwittingly imply in their attitude toward him.

It is about noontime (thus, time for lunch) when the farmer brings Gulliver to his home. Gulliver is placed upon the table (which is about thirty feet high) and given some minced meat and bread crumbs which comprise for him a quite substantial meal. Throughout his meal, the tiny Gulliver is fearful of falling off the table. He is given some liquor and, in proposing a toast before drinking it, makes the giants roar with laughter. In the course of the meal, Gulliver is almost killed by the family's ten year old son who lifts him high in the air and holds him upside down. The boy is punished for this but Gulliver, not wishing to make an enemy of the boy (for fear of what the boy-giant might do to him in the future), behaves subserviently to his young tormentor. No sooner is he saved from the mischief of the young boy, however, than Gulliver encounters yet another Brobdingnagian terror, the family cat, three times the size of an ox. Gulliver discovers that, despite the ferocious appearance of the animal, she is more fearful of the tiny man than he is of her; the same is true of the dogs. By merely strutting fearlessly in front of these animals, Gulliver is able to outface them.

The infant of the family, who treats Gulliver as one of his toys, is a more serious danger. Just as the baby is about to put him in his mouth, Gulliver screams so loudly that the child drops him. In order to quiet the child, his nurse puts him to her breast to nurse him. Gulliver is astounded at the sight of the giant woman's breast: it stands prominent six feet and is some sixteen feet in circumference. To Gulliver, who has a microscopic view of the woman, it is a most disgusting sight because all the physical details (such as freckles, discolorations, and pores) are magnified to his sight. In this disgust, he reflects that the skin of the fairest English lady, if viewed so closely, is undoubtedly quite as disgusting a sight.

Comment

Swift is directing the attack on human pride from two angles. First, to the Brobdingnagians, Gulliver is a cute toy; they respond to his actions, such as his proposing a toast, as we do to the actions of a small child. To the human reader, who is the same size as Gulliver, the effect of Swift's technique is to make us pitifully aware of our weakness and vulnerability. In the second place, Swift uses Gulliver's disgust at the sight of the skin of the Brobdingnagians to suggest that we, too (if seen in a perspective different from the one we are accustomed to measure ourselves by) are quite as disgusting physically as are these giants who, after all, do not seem disgusting to each other. Thus, it is only our pride that deludes us into thinking that we are beautiful; if we see ourselves as we really are, we find that our pride has weak foundations.

After finishing his somewhat harrowing meal, Gulliver is exhausted and is put to sleep on the farmer's wife's bed. It is some eight yards from the floor and twenty yards wide. After sleeping for two hours, Gulliver awakes, needing to relieve himself. Just as he is about to call for help so that he may be put from the bed to the floor, he is attacked by two rats each of which is the size of an English dog. Gulliver defends himself with his sword, killing one rat and wounding the other which runs off leaving a trail of blood. The tail of the dead rat measures six feet in length.

Soon after Gulliver's fight with the rats, the mistress of the house comes into the bedroom, rejoices to see that he is unharmed, disposes of the body of the dead rat, and takes Gulliver into the garden where he is finally able to attend to his physical necessities decently and privately behind two sorrel leaves.

CHAPTER II

Gulliver is given over to the care of the daughter of the house, a delightful girl nine years old who is very handy in domestic chores. Gulliver tells us that she is somewhat short for her age, attaining a height of only forty feet. The girl becomes extremely fond of Gulliver. She cares for him with great diligence and affection, treating him as a beloved pet. Gulliver is only too happy to meet with such kindness and he bestows upon the girl the pet name, Glumdalclitch, which means "little nurse." She, in turn, calls her new pet, Grildrig, which (in the language of Brobdingnag) means "mannikin" or puppet. Not only does Glumdalclitch prepare her pet's sleeping quarters, sew him shirts, wash his clothes, and dress him, but she also serves as his schoolmistress, teaching him the Brobdingnagian tongue.

Comment

Swift's satiric genius is evident in the relationship he creates between Gulliver and Glumdalclitch. Gulliver seems unaware of the blow to his dignity implied in the fact that he, a mature adult, is being cared for by a nine-year-old girl as if he were a baby or a pet; in fact, Gulliver is pleased at the care which is lavished on him.

It is not long before news of this strange, tiny creatures gets around the neighborhood. The giants are amazed at how human Gulliver seems to be but they cannot help comparing him to their splacknucks, small Brobdingnagian animals about six feet in length. One day, a friend of Gulliver's master visits the farmhouse to see the strange sight for himself. This guest has the reputation of being a miser and Gulliver is soon to find out why. The visitor, in order to observe Gulliver more closely, puts on a pair of glasses which, from Gulliver's vantage point, gives the giant a ridiculous appearance since the enormous spectacles make his eyes appear "like the full moon shining into a chamber at two windows." Gulliver laughs heartily at the moon-eyed giant who, in turn, is quite offended. The giant gets back at Gulliver by suggesting that the farmer might earn a great deal of money if he were to exhibit Gulliver to the public, charging an admission price to the viewers.

Comment

Human pride is mocked by the equally ridiculous reactions of Gulliver and the miserly giant to each other. Gulliver's foolish pride is evident in his laughter at the expense of a creature who could crush him with a touch of a finger; the giant's equally foolish pride is seen in his sensitivity to the ridicule directed against him by a creature who is barely large enough to be seen.

The farmer, much to the consternation of Glumdalclitch, takes his neighbor's advice and sets out the next morning with Gulliver to the neighboring town, intending to display the tiny man to the public. Gulliver, wounded at the thought that he is to be exhibited publicly like a zoo animal, consoles his pride with the reflection that the same fate would have befallen the King of England if he had found himself in Gulliver's situation.

The journey to town is a harrowing experience for the little man. He is held inside a little box with a door and a few air holes and is under the protection of Glumdalclitch who was considerate enough to line the inside of the box with quilting. Unfortunately, neither Glumdalclitch nor the quilting are sufficient to prevent Gulliver from being terribly shaken by the half-hour's journey; the Brobdingnagian horses cover some forty feet with each one of their steps and trot so high that, to Gulliver, the journey is like that of a ship tossed about on the waves of a great, stormy ocean.

Reaching town, Gulliver's Brobdingnagian master sets up his little show in the Green Eagle Inn and hires the town crier to advertise their arrival. Gulliver is placed on a large table in the largest room of the inn and thirty people at a time are permitted into the room to watch him perform. In actuality, he does very little: he answers questions which Glumdalclitch asks him, he flourishes his sword, he drinks a thimbleful of liquor, and he walks about the table. His audience, however, is enthralled at the sight of the miniature human being and Gulliver is forced to repeat his performance twelve times to twelve different audiences on that first day. Among one group of people, is a young boy who almost kills Gulliver by throwing a hazelnut at him: however, the nut, the size of a pumpkin, misses the little man.

Gulliver is utterly exhausted by his performance but his master gives him little rest. He announces that the show will be repeated the following week and, in the meantime, he forces Gulliver to perform at the farmhouse for the neighbors who throng to see him and are only too glad to pay for the privilege. This routine is maintained for several weeks and is so profitable that the farmer determines to take the little man into all of the great cities of the kingdom.

The troupe sets out on its journey on August 17, 1703: their general direction is toward the great metropolis, Lorbrulgrud, which is some three thousand miles from the farm. On the way, however, they make stops at eighteen towns, putting on a performance whenever a good sized audience can be gathered. The company consists of the farmer, Glumdalclitch, a boy who takes care of the luggage, and, of course, Gulliver. In about ten weeks, on October 26, the party arrives at Lorbrulgrud (which means Pride of the Universe) and settles at an inn very near the royal palace. Gulliver performs his act ten times a day on a table some sixty feet in diameter placed in a room between three and four hundred feet wide.

Gulliver tells us that by this time he has made great progress in learning the language: he understands everything that is said to him; he himself can speak fairly well and he has learned the

Brobdingnagian alphabet. Glumdalclitch teaches her pet the language from a little book she carries along with her.

Comment

Swift's depiction of the giants is complex. On the one hand, we see that they can be capable of great tenderness. This is evident in Glumdalclitch's very affectionate behavior towards Gulliver but Glumdalclitch is, after all, a child. On the other hand, her father, the farmer, is depicted as not a bad man but, rather, as insensitive to the feelings of his tiny captive. It does not occur to the farmer that Gulliver has human feelings; the farmer is quite willing to put Gulliver on display as if he were an animal and to work the poor little creature to death in order to make money from his performances. In short, the Brobdingnagians so far are neither very bad nor very good. We see them, for all their size, as capable of the same measures of kindness and selfishness as are any human beings. This picture will change somewhat as Book II continues.

CHAPTER III

So overworked is Gulliver by his master that his health begins to suffer: he is able to eat only sparingly and is almost reduced to a skeleton. His master, the farmer, observing this, realizes that Gulliver will probably die in a short time; however, instead of giving his little performer a rest, the farmer resolves to work him even harder. In this way, he hopes to make as much money as possible while Gulliver is still alive.

One day, however, a surprise visit is paid to the farmer by a Slardral, a Gentleman Usher from the court of the Brobdingnagian king. The Slardral commands the farmer to bring Gulliver to the royal court immediately for the entertainment of the Queen, who has heard the marvelous reports of the strange, tiny human animal. Upon entering the presence of the queen, Gulliver charms her by falling on his knees, kissing the tip of her little finger, answering her questions and, in every way, showing her the homage due her. Gulliver indicates that he would be happy to live at court and the Queen is so charmed by the behavior of the little man that she offers to purchase him from his master. The farmer, aware that Gulliver is not likely to live more than a month longer, is only too happy to sell him and he demands a high price, a thousand pieces of gold. The Queen agrees immediately and the money is brought to the farmer. The thousand pieces of Brobdingnagian gold, although each is the size of eight hundred European gold coins, amount to about a thousand guineas in English money. Gulliver, overjoyed at the transaction, begs the Queen one favor; to permit Glumdalclitch to stay at court with him as his nurse. The Queen agrees, much to everyone's satisfaction: the little man, Glumdalclitch herself, and the farmer (who thinks that this marks a great opportunity for his daughter to be preferred at court). After the transaction has been completed, Gulliver bids a cool farewell to his former master who almost worked him to death. Noticing Gulliver's icy manner towards the farmer, the Queen asks him the reason for it and he relates to her the manner in which he was used by the farmer. So delighted is the Queen with Gulliver's speech that she takes him, in her own hand, to her husband, the king.

Comment

The reader should note that the giants are delighted by Gulliver in much the same way that we would be delighted by a monkey who speaks fairly well and has good manners. It is because he is not quite human (to the giants) but yet does human things that they find him charming. As the book progresses, we will see Gulliver becoming more and more frustrated at the inability of the Brobdingnagians to realize that he is a real human being. We will sympathize with him in his frustration until, suddenly, Swift will play a cruel joke on us by showing us that, in fact, the giants are absolutely right about Gulliver (and about us); but this happens later.

The Queen brings her little pet to the King who, at first, reprimands his wife for becoming so involved with a splacknuck. Only on taking a closer look does he see that Gulliver resembles a human being but the King thinks that the little figure is actually an ingenious piece of clockwork, an animated doll. The King, although one of the most learned men in his nation, persists in this opinion until he hears Gulliver speak, at which time he is utterly astonished. The King refuses to believe the story Gulliver tells him about the manner in which the little man came to Brobdingnag; only after speaking privately to the farmer does the King begin to believe Gulliver's story. Still amazed, however, at the phenomenon of this diminutive mortal, the King calls in his three greatest scholars to study Gulliver and deliver an opinion as to what the little creature might be and how he might have come to be created.

The scientists come to the conclusion that Gulliver is a relplum scalcath or a freak of nature. Their opinion is based upon a rather close-minded approach to experience: they reason that, since Gulliver is not designed physically to survive in Brobdingnag, it follows that he is simply one of nature's mistakes. It does not occur to them that he might be admirably equipped to survive in another environment. Gulliver, somewhat offended at being considered a freak, hurries to explain that he is admirably adapted to life in his own country but the scholars only smile contemptuously at him. They simply refuse to believe that there is, somewhere in the world, a land of natural environment different from that of Brobdingnag. The King, however, is not satisfied with the opinions of his scholars since he sees that these opinions are based solely on preconceived assumptions; in order to satisfy himself as to the truth of Gulliver's claim to have come from a country suited to his size, the king speaks to Gulliver's former master. He elicits from him the facts of Gulliver's arrival on Brobdingnag. The King also plans to hold several discussions with Gulliver on the manner of life in Gulliver's supposed native country.

The King decrees that good care be taken of Gulliver and puts Glumdalclitch in charge of the little man. The royal cabinetmaker builds a home for Gulliver, a wooden box, sixteen feet square and twelve feet high. The ceiling is so designed that it can be opened and closed, making it possible for Gulliver's nurse to attend to the housekeeping. Soon, the room is completely furnished with chairs, tables and a bed. Gulliver asks that a lock be put on his door to keep out the rats and mice and his request is complied with. The Queen orders that clothes be made for Gulliver; the thinnest silk in the kingdom is used for his clothes but even this material is of the thickness of an English blanket. In a short while, Gulliver grows accustomed to his cumbersome new clothes, however. The clothes are designed according to Brobdingnagian fashion which resembles the Persian and the Chinese.

The Queen's fondness for Gulliver continues to grow and she demands that he dine with her at each meal. A special table is designed for him and placed to the left of the Queen's place at table. A special set of tiny silver dishes and utensils is fashioned for Gulliver; Glumdalclitch keeps Gulliver's dishes and utensils in her pocket giving them to him at his meals as he needs them. The only people at these meals are Gulliver, Glumdalclitch, the Queen, and the Queens two daughters, one sixteen, the other, thirteen and a month.

Every Wednesday (the Brobdingnagian sabbath) the entire royal family dines together in the King's chambers. At these meals, Gulliver, who has become one of the King's great favorites, sits to the left of the King. The King, on these occasions, engages Gulliver in conversations on the manners, religion, laws, government and learning of Europe. The King, an educated and intelligent man, makes wise observations on everything that Gulliver says; however, it seems to Gulliver that the prejudices of the King's education are an obstacle to that monarch's understanding of English life. Gulliver makes this observation after telling us that the King is provoked into a fit of laughter when Gulliver tells him of English life. After hearing about the dissension and strife in English politics, the King takes Gulliver in his hand and facetiously asks the little man whether he is a Whig or Tory. The King then remarks on the ridiculous thing that human grandeur is, if it can be mimicked by such "diminutive insects" as Gulliver.

Comment

It is obvious that the Brobdingnagian king responds to the idea of English political life much in the same way that we and Gulliver responded to Lilliputian politics. We thought it cute but contemptible that such little creatures could be capable of such great conflicts among themselves. To the King of Brobdingnag, the idea of Whigs and Tories, Englishmen and Frenchmen, Protestants and Catholics, all fighting amongst each other is contemptible and ridiculous, just as, to us, the disputes between the Slamecksans and Tramecksans, Big-Endians and Little-Endians, Lilliputians and Blefuscudians, were beneath contempt. The reader should be aware of the relationship that is beginning to develop now between Gulliver and the King. Swift presents the King to us as a reasonable, kind and intelligent man who finds much of what

Gulliver has to tell him about England to be beneath contempt. Gulliver, on the other hand, is offended by the king's attitude and is thus put in a position in which he must defend those aspects of English life which the king shows us to be contemptible. Gulliver, in his pride, attributes the King's failure to appreciate England's customs to shortcomings in the King's own education.

In addition to these blows to his patriotic pride, Gulliver faces some immediate physical dangers in Brobdingnag. The Queen's dwarf, a mischievous creature, grows jealous of Gulliver. Only thirty feet tall himself, he jibes at Gulliver's smallness, happy to have found someone compared to whom he himself is a giant. This is an interesting example of Brobdingnagian pride. The mischievous creature, however, because of his jealousy of Gulliver (who has become the Queen's favorite) drops the little man into a pitcher of cream on one occasion. Gulliver swims for dear life and, luckily, is rescued by Glumdalitch but not before he has swallowed a quart of cream. The dwarf is whipped and forced to drink the cream in which Gulliver was dropped. On yet another occasion, the dwarf squeezes Gulliver into a marrow bone from which the Queen has just taken the marrow. The Queen cannot restrain her laughter at Gulliver's poor plight but she has the dwarf soundly whipped for his mischief. Eventually, the Queen finds that she has to get rid of the dwarf for the sake of Gulliver's safety. She bestows the creature on a lady of high quality.

Other great dangers to Gulliver are the Brobdingnagian flies and wasps. The flies, which are the size of English larks, are a disgusting and dangerous menace to Gulliver. Sometimes they fix on his forehead and sting him painfully: sometimes, they land on his food and leave their excrement behind. On one occasion, he is attacked by a group of wasps, each as large as English partridges, with stingers an inch and a half long. Gulliver becomes quite proficient at defending himself against these Brobdingnagian insects; he cuts them down in mid-air with his sword, much to the delight of the Queen, who had begun to suspect that Gulliver was a coward.

CHAPTER IV

This short chapter is largely given over to a detailed description of some of the more interesting features of the land of Brobdingnag. Geographically, the dimensions of the kingdom are as huge as we would expect: it is about six thousand miles long and varies from three to five thousand miles in breadth. Brobdingnag is a peninsula, an enormous one, joined to the northwest parts of the North American continent. Thus, it is located in the Pacific Ocean contrary to the theories of generations of European geographers who maintained that there was no landmass between California and Japan. It is Gulliver's private opinion that the Brobdingnagian landmass balances the great continent of Tartary on the other side of the globe.

As for the land itself, it is terminated on its northeast side by a ridge of mountains thirty miles high rendered impassable by the volcanoes at their tops. On the other three sides, it is bounded by the sea. Not one seaport is to be found in Brobdingnag: this, together with the impassable mountain barrier, has excluded Brobdingnag from any dealings with the rest of the world, of which the giants are totally ignorant. However, within the country, a good deal of commerce is conducted on the nation's rivers which abound with fish. The sea fish, however, are the size of European fish and thus do not serve as food for the giants who occasionally satisfy their seafood hunger by eating whales when they are lucky enough to find the animals washed ashore. The King himself is not especially fond of whales.

There are fifty-one cities, almost one hundred walled towns, and a great number of villages in Brobdingnag, an obviously well populated nation. Lorbrulgrud, the chief city, is evenly divided into two parts by a river. The city contains six hundred thousand inhabitants and about eighty thousand houses. The city is three glongluns long (about fifty-four English miles) and two-and-a-half glongluns broad.

The King's palace is not a single building; rather, it is a collection of many edifices taking up an area seven miles in circumference. The main rooms are two hundred forty feet in height, width and length. The King provides a coach for Gulliver in which he and Glumdalclitch may go for outings. On one of these excursions into the heart of the city, Gulliver encounters some Brobdingnagian beggars who provide for him some of the most horrible sights he has ever beheld: one of the beggar women had "a cancer at her breast, swelled to a monstrous size, full of holes." Another beggar has an enormous tumor on his neck but the most disgusting sight is of the lice that crawl all over the bodies of the beggars, the sight of a giant louse turns Gulliver's stomach.

To make his traveling more comfortable, the Queen orders that a second box, about twelve feet square and ten feet high, be built for Gulliver since the large box he usually is carried in is too large for Glumdalclitch's lap and thus inconvenient for traveling about. The traveling box has three windows, a bed, two chairs, a table, and a hammock hung from its ceiling.

Gulliver is very anxious to see the chief temple of the kingdom, but after viewing it, he returns home disappointed ... for it is only three thousand feet tall. Gulliver confesses, however, that the building makes up in beauty and strength whatever it lacks in height. The walls are almost one hundred feet thick and built of stones, each of which is forty feet square. The temple is adorned with larger-than-life marble statues of the Brobdingnagian gods and emperors. Gulliver measures the little finger of one of these statues and finds it to be four-and-a-half feet in length.

Comment

Swift takes a swipe at human vanity when he tells us that Gulliver was unimpressed by a building over three thousand feet high because it was not as high proportionately as some European structures. In effect, Gulliver judges the Brobdingnagian building by European standards of size and finds the building disappointing; a patently absurd conclusion since the building, after all, is three thousand feet high!

Gulliver is most impressed with the king's kitchen but, not wishing to strain the credulity of his readers, he **refrains** from describing it. The chapter ends with Gulliver informing us that the King keeps about six hundred horses in his stables; the horses range from fifty-four to sixty feet in height.

CHAPTER V

Gulliver tells us that he is reasonably happy in Brobdingnag except for the ridiculous and troublesome accidents he encounters for reason of his tiny size. Many of these accidents occur in the Garden of the Court where Gulliver often comes out of his box and roams about freely. On one occasion, before the Queen disposes of her dwarf, both Gulliver and the dwarf are in the vicinity of a Dwarf Apple Tree; Gulliver cannot resist the temptation to make a crack about the similarity in names between the tree and the dwarf. In response to this provocation, the dwarf shakes the tree so violently that a dozen apples (each the size of a barrel) come tumbling down upon Gulliver, however, he escapes serious hurt.

On another occasion, while strolling by himself in the garden, Gulliver is caught in a sudden and violent hailstorm. Struck to the ground, he is cruelly pelted by the stones each of which is some eighteen hundred times the size of an English hailstone (or about the size of a tennis ball). Gulliver is so bruised by the storm that he is confined to his box for ten days.

A still more dangerous accident befalls Gulliver one day in the garden when a small white Spaniel belonging to one of the King's gardeners tracks down the little man's scent, finds Gulliver, picks him up in his mouth and carries him to the gardener.

The gardener, who is fond of Gulliver, is in a terrible fright, fearing the injuries that the little man might have suffered in the animal's mouth. Gulliver himself cannot speak, so great is his terror at this experience. However, as things turn out, the little man is totally unharmed, and, news of the incident is kept from the Queen, who would have been sorely displeased at Glumdalclitch for letting Gulliver out of her sight.

In fact, Glumdalclitch now does something Gulliver has long feared: she resolves never to let Gulliver out of her sight. In the past, to prevent his nurse from making such a resolution. Gulliver had concealed from her a number of accidents which had befallen him. For example, he had been attacked by a kite (a bird of prey), he had fallen into a molehill, and he had broken his right shin against the shell of a snail which he stumbled over.

Gulliver has a peculiar feeling towards the birds who pop about in the garden; he is not sure whether he is pleased or mortified by the fact that the smaller birds are not at all afraid of him. Actually, a thrush is brash enough to snatch, from Gulliver's hand, a piece of cake the little man is eating for breakfast. For his amusement, Gulliver attempts to catch these birds but he is never successful; when he approaches them, they peck at him. One day, however, he stuns a linnet with a blow from a cudgel and seizes the stunned bird by the neck. Exhilarated by his triumph, Gulliver runs with his captive to Glumdalclitch to show her what he has accomplished, so proud is he of it. The bird, however, regains consciousness and starts beating Gulliver with its wings. One of the Brobdingnagian servants takes the bird from Gulliver and wrings its neck. The next day, it is prepared for Gulliver's dinner, the linnet being the size of an English swan.

Comment

These accidents which befall Gulliver, and which are described in such detail, serve a number of purposes. First, they reinforce the reader's impressions of the great disparity in size between Gulliver (whose scale of measurement is ours) and the Brobdingnagians. Second, we see that Gulliver is almost unconsciously forced by the physical disparity between himself and his masters to behave in a childish way: he teases the dwarf, he seeks Glumdalclitch's praise for capturing a bird (just as a child seeks the praise of his mother). Third, despite the fact of his incredible physical predicament, he makes ridiculous (to the giants) and pathetic (to us, the readers) attempts to preserve his dignity as a mature, English adult.

Gulliver is a great favorite of the maids of honor of the Queen's court. They invite Glumdalclitch to bring him to their apartments. One of their chief amusements is to strip the little naked man and lay him at full length on their breasts, a practice which disgusts him because of his extreme sensitivity to the odors given off by even the cleanest Brobdingnagian flesh. He reflects that the most fastidious English ladies would smell as bad to a keen enough nose. In fact, Gulliver recalls that a Lilliputian friend of his once told him that he smelled bad on an occasion when he had exercised vigorously.

Gulliver is offended further that these Brobdingnagian girls dress and undress in front of him and think nothing of urinating in his presence. He is offended because to be treated so familiarly by the girls indicates that they think him to be a person of no consequence. He is far from delighted at the sight of their naked bodies whose every defect is magnified to his sight: he sees their moles, as large as a trencher, and is disgusted by their bodily hair, thick as packthreads. Most disgusting to him is the enormous quantity of urine they discharge, often as much as two barrels full and he was particularly annoyed by an otherwise delightful girl of sixteen whose favorite game it is to set him astride one of her nipples; this is in addition to other tricks which he excuses himself from detailing for us.

| Comment

Swift is accomplishing a number of things in this account of the sexual play of the Brobdingnagian maids of honor. First, it is a swipe at the moral behavior of the ladies of the English court. Second, it represents another attack on human pride; it is an attack based upon the feelings of disgust Swift arouses in us at our own physicality. Seen closely, we are far from beautiful; nor do we smell nice.

One day, Gulliver is treated to the spectacle of a public execution. The doomed man's head is cut off with a forty foot sword and so great a quantity of blood spurts from the beheaded carcass that Gulliver is reminded of the great fountains at Versailles. Gulliver is a mile from the scene of the execution but is, nevertheless, startled by the bounce taken by the disembodied head as it falls upon the floor of the scaffold.

In her conversations with Gulliver, the Queen has often heard him talk of his life on the sea and it occurs to her that her little man might enjoy the exercise of rowing. She offers to have her carpenter build Gulliver a boat proportioned to his size and to provide a place for him to row. In ten days, the carpenter builds a lovely little pleasure boat with facilities for oars and sails, able to hold conveniently eight Europeans. As a place to row his boat, a wooden trough (three hundred feet long, fifty broad, and eight deep), is designed and built for Gulliver. The trough is kept in an outer room of the palace. The Queen and her ladies are delighted by the sight of the little man rowing his little boat: occasionally, for the sake of variety, Gulliver hoists his sail and the ladies create a breeze with their fans. Gulliver then entertains them with his skill in navigating his little craft.

Comment

The reader will notice that, in supplying Gulliver with a toy for his amusement, the Queen has in effect made of him a toy for her own amusement.

The greatest danger Gulliver experiences in Brobdingnag is from a monkey (the size of an elephant) who lives in the Court. The mischievous animal spies Gulliver inside his box and, reaching in through the opened door, the animal seizes Gulliver and draws him forth. The monkey behaves affectionately to Gulliver, stroking the little man's face as if Gulliver were himself an infant monkey (for which the animal seems to have mistaken him). He also causes Gulliver great pain by squeezing him tightly. As Glumdalclitch enters the room, the monkey leaps out of the window with his captive and clambers up to the ridge of a nearby building some five hundred yards from the ground. While the people below go about collecting ladders, the monkey holds Gulliver like a baby in one of his forepaws and, with the other, feeds his captive, cramming into his mouth some food he carries about him in a bag. The rescuers finally apply their ladders and drive the frightened monkey away; the animal leaves Gulliver on the ledge at a dizzy height. A young boy soon climbs up and, placing Gulliver in the pocket of his breeches, brings the little man down safely.

While no serious harm befalls Gulliver on this adventure, he is so bruised by the monkey's grip and so nauseous from the food he is forced to eat that he is obliged to keep to his bed for two weeks; but by far the greatest damage done is to the little man's pride. The giants, although they are genuinely concerned for his safety, cannot forbear laughing at his plight. To them, the little man's helplessness before the affectionate monkey is hilarious. Gulliver makes it clear to the king that, if he were attacked by monkeys in England, he could easily dispatch twelve of them at a time but these declarations of his courage only serve to make the giants laugh more heartily (though good-naturedly) at Gulliver.

On yet another occasion, Gulliver provides the court with some mirth at his own expense. While walking in a field, he spies a pile of cow dung and attempts to make a running leap over it for the sake of the exercise. However, the poor little fellow jumps short and lands in the dung up to his knees. He is wiped clean by the footman but, for several days, is the laughing stock of the court.

CHAPTER VI

In this leisure at the court, Gulliver proves himself to be quite an ingenious craftsman. After the King's barber shaves the king one day, Gulliver collects about forty or fifty stumps of the monarch's hair, inserts them into a fine piece of wood and, in this way, fashions a comb for himself; the stumps of the king's beard being strong enough to serve as the teeth of a comb. On another occasion, he asks the Queen's cabinet-maker to fashion two chair frames the right size for the little man. Then, taking a few strands of the Queen's hair, Gulliver weaves them around the frames and fashions, in this way, two chairs just like English cane chairs; these he presents as a gift to the Queen who is most pleased with them. She keeps them in her curio cabinet. For his little nurse, Glumdalclitch, Gulliver weaves a purse with the remaining hairs of the Queen. The purse is five feet long but not strong enough to bear the weight of Brobdingnagian coins.

The King is a great music lover and he often invites Gulliver to attend the court concerts. Gulliver finds, however, that the music is so deafening that he cannot enjoy it unless he withdraws into his box, shuts the doors and windows, and draws the curtains. Noting the King's fondness for music and wishing to please the good man, Gulliver devises an entertainment in which he succeeds in playing a tune on a Brobdingnagian piano. He has a bench placed four feet below the keyboard and, with two round sticks in his hands, he runs back and forth along the bench striking the keys with his sticks. The Brobdingnagian piano is some sixty feet long; obviously the little man has no great range of notes, but he manages to strike out melodies by using only sixteen keys. The process, however, is the most violent exercise Gulliver has ever had.

Comment

Gulliver, in fashioning the chairs for the Queen and performing on the giant piano for the King, is attempting to impress the royal couple with his ingenuity and craftsmanship. He feels a need to impress them as a way of asserting his dignity. The reader, however, cannot help but smile at his efforts; instead of standing as examples of adult achievement, they remind us of the efforts a child makes to win the approval of his parents.

The King has many conversations with Gulliver, chiefly on European, particularly English, life, manners, government and history. However, the King is singularly unimpressed with what he learns; in fact, he makes no secret of his contempt for the little creatures about whom Gulliver tells him. Gulliver, frustrated by the King's attitude, makes one final attempt to better the monarch's opinion of the English; the little man gives the King an account of the English government which, he feels, cannot fail to impress the giant King.

Gulliver begins by singing the praises of the House of Lords and of the noblemen who sit in that chamber. He tells the King of their ancient lineage and of the extraordinary "care taken of their education in Arts, and Arms, to qualify them for being Counselors born to the King and the Kingdom." Sitting side by side with these illustrious noblemen in the House of Lords are the Bishops who look after the Church and the moral welfare of the people; these Bishops are distinguished by the sanctity of their lives and "the Depth of their erudition." They are "indeed the spiritual fathers of the Clergy and the People."

In much the same manner, Gulliver goes on to describe, in the most glorious terms, the members of the House of Commons, the Courts of Justice and the prudent management of the English treasury. Finally, he brings his description of English life to a close with a brief historical account of events and affairs of the last one hundred years in England.

Comment

Gulliver, desperately trying to preserve his dignity, makes every attempt to change the King's poor opinion of his people and his country. Thus, when he describes the English government, he describes it not as it really is, but as it might be ideally. Swift's satiric genius is quite evident here for he invites the reader to contrast the actual state of the English government with the ideal described by Gulliver.

Throughout these conversations, of which there are five, the Brobdingnagian King takes frequent notes and makes memorandums of the questions he intends to ask Gulliver about Gulliver's account of English life. On the occasion of their sixth conversation, the King directs a number of sharp observations and critical questions at Gulliver. It does not take him very long to see that the government and the country described by Gulliver are, in almost every way, corrupt; that the noblemen were more often gamblers than counselors, the clergy more often venal than holy, the courts more often in the service of injustice than of justice. As for the last hundred years of English history, the King characterizes them as "an heap of conspiracies, rebellions, murders, massacres, revolutions, banishments; the very worst effects that avarice, faction, hypocrisy, perfidiousness, cruelty, rage, madness, hatred, envy, lust, malice and ambition could produce." The King takes Gulliver into his hands and strokes him gently with an attitude of condescending pity, like that of a tender parent towards a mischievous and bewildered child. Then the King delivers a lecture to Gulliver, in which he sums up his opinions on the English nation and the English people. He tells Gulliver that the English obviously, at one time, possessed a government and a way of life which might have been tolerable but that it is clear to him that the English institutions and people had been corrupted in the course of their history.

Comment

The reader will note that the last mentioned opinion of the King is identical with Gulliver's own judgment of the Lilliputians. In effect, Gulliver is being told that his country is as morally corrupt as is Lilliput.

The King continues by telling Gulliver that, from what he has observed in Gulliver's own account of his nation, he cannot help but conclude that the English are "the most pernicious race of little odious vermin that nature ever suffered to crawl upon the surface of the earth."

Comment

Until this point in Book II, the attitude of the King towards Gulliver has been one of playful affection for a weaker and helpless (but amusing) little creature; but, now, the King is genuinely shocked and dismayed by what he has discovered about English life and English people. The King takes a serious and disdainful tone towards the little man and, suddenly, we see that Gulliver's physical smallness is symbolic of his moral smallness as compared to the giant King. The giants, we are forced to see are better as well as bigger than Gulliver and since we, the readers, have been tricked by Swift into identifying and sympathizing with Gulliver throughout his tribulations among the giants, the cruelest joke (in a sense) is on us; for we are Gulliver. In the eyes of the giants, we would be as bad as he is; our government, as bad as his. All the moral censure we had formerly directed against the despicable Lilliputians we now must direct back against ourselves. It is on this melancholy note that Chapter VI ends.

CHAPTER VII

Gulliver tells us that, if it were not for his love for truth, he would have concealed from us the last part of his story, that part in which the giant King so unmercifully condemns the English nation. Gulliver makes it clear, however, that, in his conversations with the King, he attempted to elude the most embarrassing questions put to him about English life and that, in general, he would stretch the truth as much as possible in order to make the English appear in the most favorable light. He did this because, he firmly believed the opinion of the ancient historian Dionysius Halicarnassensis who held that a man should hide the faults and emphasize the virtues of his native country. Yet, no matter how he tried, all his attempts to impress the Brobdingnagian King were futile.

Gulliver tells us, however, that the King's failure to think well of the English (that is, of us, the readers) is the result of that monarch's isolation from other nations. Gulliver contends that the King's attitude is shot through with prejudices and a narrow-mindedness not to be encountered in England or Europe; and, to show us that the King's notions of virtue and vice were too foolish to serve as standards for ourselves, Gulliver tells of the following incident:

Gulliver makes one more attempt to win the respect of the King, he describes, for the monarch, the European invention of gunpowder and its use in cannons; furthermore, he offers to supervise for the King the construction of a cannon. This would be a weapon with which the King could easily intimidate his subjects into accepting him as the absolute master of their lives, liberties and fortunes. Gulliver describes, in bloody detail, the power of such a weapon: he tells how the cannonballs can "destroy whole ranks of an army at once, batter the strongest walls to the ground, sink down ships with a thousand men in each, divide hundreds of bodies in the middle, rip up pavements, tear houses to pieces, dash out the brains of all who came near." Surely, with weaponry like this, the King could become an absolute tyrant.

The King, however, listens to Gulliver in horror. Far from wishing to use such weapons to become absolute master of his kingdom, the monarch says that he would rather lose half his realm than possess weapons of such terror. Furthermore, the giant King expresses amazement that so "impotent and groveling an insect" as Gulliver could entertain such inhuman ideas and express them in so casual a manner as to seem unaware of and unmoved by the scenes of blood and destruction and human suffering caused by those horrible weapons. Gulliver, however, is even more amazed by this attitude of the King; he cannot believe that a man in his right mind would choose to renounce such instruments of power as Gulliver has offered him. The little Englishman, dumbfounded, attributes the King's attitude to "narrow principles and short views."

Comment

Nowhere is Swift's satiric genius more evident than in this section. It is now painfully clear to us that Gulliver is morally (as well as physically) inferior to the Brobdingnagians. It is Gulliver, not the giants, who shows himself to be unmindful of the horror and suffering implied in his proposal to the King. It is the King, the figure of great physical strength, who has all the kindness and compassion for human suffering. The reader will also note that Swift is implicating us; it is all too clear that we, along with Gulliver, find it hard to understand the King's refusal to accept those weapons which might give him so much power and Gulliver who, in Lilliput, was horrified at the tiny Emperor's desire to completely subjugate the Blefuscudians, here, in Brobdingnag, is dumbfounded at the King's refusal to become a tyrant. Thus, the reversal is complete: here in Brobdingnag, Gulliver is no better than the cruel and odious Lilliputians he had despised when he was a "giant."

After being humiliated by the Brobdingnagian king, Gulliver makes some petulant observations on the education of the giant folk. It is his opinion that the giants are intellectually inferior to the Europeans since their learning consists only of Morality, History, Poetry and Mathematics (what we call the liberal arts). He particularly scorns the fact that the Brobdingnagians do not indulge in abstract learning; thus, they study mathematics but only in order to apply it usefully in life to the improvement of agriculture and the mechanical arts.

Comment

What Gulliver scorns, Swift would have praised as we shall see more particularly in Book III in which Swift attacks a society of mad scholars who pursue abstract learning. Swift would have heartily approved of Brobdingnagian education.

The giants do not possess large libraries; they are not a very bookish people. The King's library contains only about a thousand volumes. Occasionally, Gulliver reads a book in the King's library, a difficult task, physically, since the books are easily twice Gulliver's size. He has to prop the book against a wall and stand on top of a ladder in order to read the top lines, descending step by step as he approaches the bottom of the page.

One of the books Gulliver looks into is a popular moral treatise, much in the European vein. In it, the Brobdingnagian author muses on the weakness of man, his vulnerability and mortality, and concludes that man is one of the poorest creatures of God's making.

Comment

It is amusing to creatures of our size to see giants write about themselves and their weaknesses in the same manner as we muse about ours. If a giant conceives of himself as being weak and subject to all manner of natural injury, how weak and destructible, then, are we?

The King maintains an army of about one hundred seventy-six thousand foot soldiers and thirty-two thousand cavalrymen but this is not a standing army; it is, rather, an army of civilians who are on ready alert and, thus, cannot be used by the King against his own countrymen in order to intimidate them. The necessity for an army stemmed from the days of internal conflicts and civil wars which bedeviled Brobdingnag during the reign of the present King's grandfather. These conflicts, however, were settled during the reign of that King in a compact which settled the disputes between the people, the nobility and the King. Thus, the army has not been called upon for some time, although it drills regularly.

Comment

Swift is trying to show us that Brobdingnag is a stable nation of free people. They are not perfect but are about as good as people and nations can be. The King governs and maintains order but is no tyrant. The nation is not bedeviled by civil strife. Swift means us to contrast the kingdom of Brobdingnag with those of Lilliput and England.

CHAPTER VIII

As it becomes more and more difficult for Gulliver to maintain his human dignity before the giants, he begins to long for home and to bend his thoughts in the direction of rescue. His wish to escape is intensified when he learns that the King has ordered that a careful watch be maintained for any stray humans like Gulliver. It is the King's wish that a female be found so that the breed may be propagated. This sought repels Gulliver for he recognizes that his descendants in Brobdingnag would be treated like pets, not like men. Thus, unable to convince the giants that he deserves to be treated like a man (not a pet), Gulliver longs for England where he can be among those of his own kind.

Comment

Our feelings toward Gulliver are ambiguous here. On the one hand, we recognize that (compared to the giants) he is morally inferior to them. If the giants are men, then Gulliver is a poor physical and moral imitation of man and, therefore, the giants are justified in not taking him seriously. On the other hand, however, we cannot help but identify with Gulliver and sympathize with his plight because we, after all, are his size: we are not Brobdingnagians. Thus, though we recognize that he does not deserve the respect he would like to have from the giants, we admire his own misguided sense of his human dignity.

Sometime after Gulliver had been in Brobdingnag for two years, the royal couple take him with them on a journey to the city of Fanflasnic which is located some eighteen English miles from the sea. Gulliver is anxious to see the ocean but his nurse, Glumdalclitch, has become ill on the journey to Fanflasnic and cannot accompany him. Reluctantly, in response to Gulliver's pleading, the girl disobeys the Queen's orders never to let Gulliver out of her sight. She consents to Gulliver's demands and puts the little man in the charge of a page, a young boy who has, on occasions, looked after Gulliver in the past. Upon reaching the seashore, however, the page puts Gulliver (who is in his traveling box) down and runs off to play by himself. Gulliver, tired, from the trip, takes a nap.

Suddenly, the little man is awakened by a jolt. As he looks out of the window of his box, he sees that he is being lifted high into the air. He hears the sound of flapping wings and realizes that his box is being carried away by an enormous eagle. Soon, the eagle is pursued by two other birds and, in order to escape them, drops his burden. Luckily, Gulliver's box lands in the sea, where it floats having sustained almost no damage from the impact.

Now occur some of the most despairing moments of Gulliver's life. As he takes stock of his situation, he realizes that he is doomed to a cruel death; even if his box manages to hold out the sea, he will die a death of cold and starvation. He is occupied with these thoughts for about four hours when he begins to perceive that his box is being tugged. He begins to hope for some kind of rescue; using one of his chairs as a ladder, he removes the small lid at the top of his box and begins to call for help in all of the languages he knows. At the same time, he waves his handkerchief at the end of a stick. Suddenly, after about an hour's time, the motion of the box stops abruptly with a jolt and he perceives that it is being hoisted. Imagine his joy when he discovers that he is being lifted aboard an English ship!

Gulliver is taken aboard ship while the sailors stand about in amazement. The captain of the ship, Mr. Thomas Wilcocks of Shropshire, perceives that Gulliver is in great need of rest and sees to it that the poor fellow goes to sleep. Some hours later, at eight in the evening, Gulliver awakens and sits down to dine with the captain, who asks many questions about the peculiar circumstances in which he was discovered. The captain, of course, thinks that Gulliver is a madman when he hears the fantastic story about the land of the giants; not only is Gulliver's story fantastic, but his behavior is queer because he has difficulty in adjusting to the normal sizes of men and objects. The sailors, for example, appear to be pygmies to Gulliver (who has just spent two years among giants) and his actions indicate that he is afraid to crush them. In almost every respect, his actions and stories seem to be those of a lunatic. The captain is convinced that Gulliver is not only mad but also a criminal who had been set adrift to die at sea.

Comment

Swift is most skillful in depicting the difficulties involved in Gulliver's return to a world of human sizes and proportions. In two years, the man has grown accustomed to the proportions of a world of giants and Swift is most ingenious in conveying Gulliver's awkwardness in his first dealings with a world of normal human proportions.

Luckily, Gulliver has brought with him many mementos of his stay in Brobdingnag. (These articles he kept in his box all the time so it does not strain our credulity to discover that he has them with him at this point.) In order to convince the captain of the truth of his story, Gulliver shows him the comb he had made from the stumps of the king's beard along with another comb made of the same materials fixed into a paring of the Queen's thumbnail. In addition to these curious items, there are needles and pins from a foot to a half yard in length, four wasp stings, some combings of the Queen's hair, a gold ring which fits over Gulliver's head, a corn from a Maid of Honor's toe, a footman's tooth (a foot long) and Gulliver's breeches made of the skin of a Brobdingnagian mouse. Upon seeing these trinkets, the captain is forced to admit the truth of his passenger's incredible story. Gulliver offers the captain his choice of any one of these curiosities as a gift; he chooses the footman's tooth.

About nine months after his escape from Brobdingnag, Gulliver reaches England after making stops at Tonquin and the Cape of Good Hope. Upon reaching his native land, Gulliver immediately sets out for his home in Redriff where he has all kinds of difficulties in adjusting to the sights of the houses, animals and people, all of which seem so tiny to him that he fears that he will trample them. He almost gets into several fights with people who take offense at his insistence that they clear the way for him, a demand he makes only because he is afraid that he will hurt them.

The good man is enthusiastically greeted when he reaches home although, at first, his family thinks that he has lost his wits. In a little while, they adjust to reach other but Gulliver's wife, seeing the effects of her husband's latest adventure, insists that he never go to sea again. She is to be disappointed in her hope, as we shall see in Part III.

ANALYSIS OF BOOK II

In Swift's treatment of Gulliver's adventures among the giants we see the art of **satire** practiced to perfection. Swift's trick is to force us, the readers, to identify with Gulliver and then to show us how Gulliver and we are morally inferior to the giants.

What then are the qualities which make the giants our betters? What can we learn from them?

First, it is important to note that the Brobdingnagians are far from perfect. We see from the actions of Gulliver's first master, the farmer, that they can be capable of avarice and unfeeling exploitation. The faults of the farmer, however, are to be contrasted with the virtues of the King who represents the highest pitch of moral development we have yet encountered in *Gulliver's Travels*.

Most prominent of all King's virtues in his lack of pride, his awareness of the limitations of mankind. Thus, he is horrified at

Gulliver's description of the power of gunpowder and refuses Gulliver's offer of the weapon because he realizes that it is too powerful to be put into the hands of so imperfect a creature as man. How correct he becomes painfully evident when we analyze Gulliver's unmindful description of the cruel power of artillery: the little man describes the destructive potential of a cannon without showing any awareness of the human pain and terror such a weapon creates. Exactly because the King is aware that man is not likely to put the power of gunpowder to good uses does he refuse to accept the weapon.

In so doing, he also refuses one of the "benefits" he might derive from the possession of such a weapon: absolute control over the lives of his subjects. The reader should contrast this King's attitude toward tyranny with that of the Lilliputian Emperor who grew angry at Gulliver's refusal to bring the Blefuscudians totally under his power. Ironically, Gulliver in Brobdingnag unwittingly adopts the attitude he so thoroughly despised in the Lilliputian Emperor. Gulliver now thinks that the Brobdingnagian King is foolish in not wishing to take upon himself the powers of a tyrant.

Because of the virtues of the King, Brobdingnag enjoys that Swift would have considered the ideal political life: it is a nation of free people under the leadership of a wise and benevolent king. Nowhere in Brobdingnag do we find the corruption and indignity that comprised Lilliputian political life. Only when a monarch possesses absolute and arbitrary power do we find such outrages as rope dancing and crawling under sticks as means of political advancement.

The Brobdingnagians are also a very practical people. They study only those subjects which are of direct value in improving their moral lives and in providing decent living conditions.

Without pride, aware of his limitations, with no desire to gather to himself a tyrant's power, and eminently practical, the Brobdingnagian King is Swift's depiction of what it is in man's power to become. Unfortunately, Gulliver represents, in Book II, Swift's depiction of how far man is from reaching that goal, and the reason for Gulliver's moral bankruptcy is his pride. Under the pressure of Brobdingnagian scrutiny, all that is bad in Gulliver is forced to the surface as the little man makes vain effort after vain effort to prove his worth to the giants. Had he tried to learn from the King instead of attempting to impress him, Book II would not have ended on so melancholy a note.

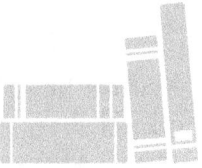

GULLIVER'S TRAVELS

TEXTUAL ANALYSIS

BOOK III

INTRODUCTORY NOTE

Most critics agree that Book II is the least satisfactory of the four major sections of the *Travels*. We are disappointed with it because it is a disjointed series of adventures in which Gulliver takes part only in name. Somehow, in Gulliver's experiences in Book III, we seem to hear Swift and not Gulliver doing the talking. Thus, we miss the rich interplay between the character of Gulliver and ourselves, the readers; an interplay through which the satiric meaning of Books I and II was created.

In some ways, Book III is the hardest for the modern reader to understand, not because it is especially difficult but because it is based upon an attitude which is alien to us. In Book III, Swift is largely concerned with investigating human pride as it manifests itself in man's scientific pursuits. Swift attacks science, an attack which is difficult for us to sympathize with. Swift tries to show us that science is not a moral pursuit, that it leads to one's alienation from what is important and real in life, and ultimately represents a kind of moral madness. In evaluating Swift's position, strange as it is to us, perhaps we stand to benefit by arriving at an understanding of the problems science has caused us; certainly, our common uncritical view of science as merely the source of untold blessings can stand the buffets of a satirical genius however uncongenial that genius may be.

CHAPTER I

About ten days after Gulliver returns home from Brobdingnag, he is paid a series of visits by Captain William Robinson, a Cornish man and commander of the ship Hopewell. In the past, Gulliver had been a surgeon of another ship under the command of Captain Robinson. The purpose of Robinson's visits is to convince Gulliver to sail with him on a voyage to the East Indies. He promises Gulliver terms which our friend cannot refuse: he is offered double his usual salary, he will have another surgeon under his authority, and he will have a share in the ship's command. With some difficulty, Gulliver succeeds in getting his wife's consent to his new voyage and, in two months, on August 5, 1706, he sets out.

On April 11, 1707, the ship arrives at St. George, stopping there for three weeks to refresh the crew, many of whom are sick. The ship then sets out for Tonquin where Captain Robinson is forced to keep his ship for several months in order to wait for some goods which have not arrived on schedule. In order to defray some of the costs of his protracted stay at Tonquin, the captain buys another ship, a sloop. He loads it with goods which he hopes to sell to the neighboring islands and he puts Gulliver in command of the small ship on its trading mission.

Three days out of Tonquin, Gulliver's sloop runs into a storm which rages for five days, driving the ship in a northeasterly, then easterly direction. Suddenly, on the tenth day out of Tonquin, Two pirate ships appear, chase Gulliver's ship and overtake it with little trouble. The two pirate crews board the sloop, bind Gulliver and his crew and search the ship for booty. Among the pirate crews is a Dutchman who seems to have some authority although he is not the captain of either ship. The Dutchman, recognizing his captives as Englishmen, promises them a cruel death, swearing in an unprovoked rage that the English sailors will be tied back-to-back and thrown into the sea. Gulliver appeals to the Dutchman, as a European and a Christian, to be merciful but the plea is in vain; it serves only to provoke further the Dutchman's causeless fury.

However, the Japanese captain of one of the pirate ships approaches Gulliver and, after asking him several questions, promises the Englishman that he and his men will not be killed. Upon hearing this, Gulliver turns to the Dutchman and berates him for having less mercy than the heathen Japanese. This only infuriates the Dutchman who is able to prevail on his captain to condemn Gulliver to an even crueler death than had been first proposed: while his men are taken aboard the pirate ships, Gulliver is set adrift in a small lifeboat with paddles, a sail, and four days' provisions (increased to eight on the generous impulse of the Japanese captain). As Gulliver drifts away from the pirate ship, the Dutchman (standing on its deck) hurls at Gulliver all the curses and injurious terms which his language contains.

Comment

Gulliver's adventures in Brook III thus begin with a frankly unflattering account of the barbarity and cruelty one finds in a native of civilized, Christian Europe. It is as if the Brobdingnagian King's opinion of Europeans is validated here in the behavior of the Dutchman.

Shortly after he is set adrift, Gulliver observes, through his pocket glass, a group of islands off to the southeast. In three hours, he reaches the nearest of these islands and, with the ingenuity we have come to expect of him, he finds some birds' eggs and roasts and eats them for his supper. He also devises for himself a shelter beneath a rock and manages to secure for himself a good night's sleep.

For the next five days, he explores all of the islands in the group and settles on the last one, a land of rocky, barren aspect, full of caves with only sparse and occasional patches of grass. He gathers all the eggs he can find, devises a shelter for himself within a cave, gathers dry grass and seaweed for fuel and, having done all this, sits down and contemplates the misery of his predicament, wondering about the manner in which he will meet his inevitable death.

As he is thinking these thoughts, he notices that the sun, which had been shining brightly, grows suddenly dark and obscure. He perceives an enormous opaque body cover the face of the sum. To his astonishment, this object seems to be suspended in the air and moving towards him. As he observes it more closely, it becomes quite clear that it is nothing other than a flying island with a flat bottom and sloping sides! Moving up and down the sides of the island are large numbers of people.

As the island moves closer to him, Gulliver is able to distinguish several levels of galleries and stairs along its sides. In the lowest gallery, people seem to be fishing with long angling rods. Seeing some hope for rescue, Gulliver does all he can to attract the attention of the islanders and he begins to perceive that a crowd is forming on that part of the island nearest to him. They see him. The island is maneuvered towards him and one of the men calls to him in a language which resembles Italian. Gulliver begs to be taken up and the islanders signal him to walk down to the beach. The island is then positioned properly above him and a seat is lowered down to him at the bottom of the chain. Gulliver fixes himself in it and is drawn up by pulleys to the island.

CHAPTER II

As he alights upon the flying island, Gulliver is surrounded by a crowd of people who gape at him with wonder and astonishment but he is no less amazed by them. Certainly, they are the most singular people he has ever seen. "Their heads were all reclined to the right, or the left; one of their eyes turned inward, and the other directly up to the zenith. Their outward garments were adorned with the figures of suns, moons and stars, interwoven with those of fiddles, flutes, harps, trumpets, guitars, harpsichords and many more instruments of music unknown to us in Europe." ... so Gulliver describes them.

The people of the flying island who wear these strange costumes are scientists, mathematicians and musicians. They are a people given to such intense and constant speculation that they are incapable of conversing with others or among themselves and cannot even walk about safely; for they are so lost in their thoughts that they forget that they are being spoken to and that they must respond. They lose sight of the obstacles in their paths and are thus in danger of falling down every precipice or tripping over every obstacle in the streets. In order to avoid the dangers and inconveniences of such a constant state of intense cogitation, the scientists and mathematicians employ servants known as flappers. These flappers carry a bag containing little pebbles. When the Laputians (for such is the name of the inhabitants of the flying island, Laputa) try to engage in conversation with one another, they must be reminded to listen and reply. This is the function of the flapper who gently strikes the mouth of him who is to speak while another flapper strikes the right ear of him who is to listen. The flappers do this with the bags containing the pebbles. In this way, the Laputians are temporarily prevented from becoming lost in their thoughts and it is only thanks to the flappers that conversation is at all possible on Laputa. A good example of the effects of such intense thought is seen when a few of these people conduct Gulliver to the royal palace. Several times on their way to the palace, the Laputians forget why they are going there and they leave Gulliver to himself as they become lost in their thoughts. Only the constant reminders of their flappers bring them back to their senses from time to time.

Comment

In this hilarious, if somewhat overdrawn account of the mad society of mathematicians and scientists, Swift is depicting the harmful effects of abstruse speculation. Swift is trying to make us see that abstract speculation is not the best application of our God-given reason. The reader will recall how free the Brobdingnagians were of this sort of thing. Swift's point is that people who are given to speculation on natural phenomena, merely for the sake of speculation, are likely to be removed from real life and unable to conduct themselves within a social environment. Thus, the Laputians are constantly lost in their own thoughts and are unable to communicate with one another unless they are reminded to listen and to speak.

Gulliver is led into the presence of the King of the flying island. The King, seated on his throne, is so wrapped up in a problem that more than an hour passes before he notices Gulliver. In front of the throne is a large table filled with globes and spheres and mathematical instruments of all kinds. When the King has solved his problem, one of his flappers strikes his mouth and the other his right ear thus signaling him to get ready to converse. The King addresses Gulliver and a flapper approaches Gulliver and strikes him gently on the right ear but Gulliver makes it understood that he does not need to be flapped in order to converse. He later discovers that the King and the whole court have a low opinion of his intelligence; they feel that anyone who does not need a flapper cannot be much of a thinker.

The King and Gulliver do not have a satisfactory conversation because neither can understand the other's language. The King, however, is not hospitable; he has prepared a room for Gulliver in the palace and has asked four persons of quality to dine with Gulliver. The dinner is most interesting, not because of the company but because the various foods are cut and served in the form of triangles, rhomboids, parallelograms, fiddles, flutes, oboes and harps. The bread is cut into cones, cylinders and several other mathematical figures.

After the dinner, Gulliver's company withdraws and a person, attended by a flapper, calls on Gulliver. The King has sent him to teach Gulliver the language. The man's books are all about the sun, moon, stars and music. Gulliver makes lists of words and diligently studies his new vocabulary. Within a few days, he begins to be able to use the new language haltingly. He finds that his knowledge of mathematics (such as it is) is a great help in his learning the Laputian phraseology which is replete with mathematical and musical terms. The Laputians express all of their ideas, no matter their subject, in the terms of mathematics and music. Thus, a beautiful woman would be described in terms of circles, ellipses, parallelograms and other such forms. The King's kitchen is full of all sorts of mathematical and musical instruments which serve as the models according to which the meat is to be cut and served.

The King orders a tailor to measure Gulliver for a suit of clothes and Gulliver is most surprised at the tailor's method of taking a man's measure. Scorning the tape measure, the tailor measures Gulliver's height with a quadrant and then, with a ruler and compasses, describes the dimensions and outlines of Gulliver's body. The tailor sets his calculations down on paper and, six days later, returns with a very poorly made suit, quite out of shape. Gulliver is comforted by the fact that such accidents are very common in Laputa. For example, the houses there are very poorly built, with leaning walls and scarcely a right angle to be seen in any apartment. Gulliver attributes these inefficiencies to the fact that the Laputians scorn the practical applications of their sciences; their workmen would rather theorize than measure. Consequently, Gulliver concludes that he never encountered a people more awkward and clumsy in the common affairs of life. Furthermore, they are rather dull, being completely devoid of imagination, fancy and invention. Their thoughts are entirely given over to mathematics and music. Besides these two subjects, the only other passionate concern of the Laputians is politics, a subject with which they are totally unqualified to deal.

Comment

Laputa is beginning to appear as some kind of mad society, a land in which human reason is incorrectly used and is thus of no help where it is most sorely needed ... in the management of one's daily life. Thus, the Laputians are excellent mathematicians but there is not a decently built house or properly fitted suit of clothes in the kingdom. The only non-mathematical, non-musical area of Laputian interest is politics, a subject for which the people are eminently unqualified. Indeed, as we shall soon see, they have made a mess of their own political lives.

A noteworthy thing about the Laputians is that they take no comfort from their mathematical and scientific achievements: in fact, their knowledge of astronomy serves only to infuse a persistent and daily anxiety into their lives for they are constantly conceiving of the possibility that the world will be destroyed, either by collision with comets or by the burning out of the sun or by other such eventualities. In fact, at the time Gulliver was their guest, they had calculated that the world would end in thirty-one years when it would pass through the tail of a comet.

The women of Laputa, however, are in no way like their men; the Laputian wives are gay, vivacious women who bridle at their confinement on the flying island. They deceive their husbands at every opportunity and are extremely pleased when they are visited by strangers from the land of Balnibarbi (the island over which Laputa constantly hovers.) Since their husbands are always lost in thought, a lively Laputian woman has no difficulty conducting love affairs; often, right in front of her husband. The greatest wish of the Laputian women is to leave the island. It is very difficult to get permission for this since most of those who leave try never to return. Once, the wife of the Prime Minister left the flying island for a visit to Balnibarbi and did not return for several months. When the Laputians searched for her, she was found to be living with an old and deformed menial servant who beat her regularly. Yet, she returned to Laputa much against her will and, on the first opportunity she had, she escaped again to Balnibarbi and took up with her old man again; even he was better than life in the mad world of Laputa.

Comment

We are beginning to see that the mad scientists of Laputa are, in almost every way, cut off from real life. They are obviously incapable of love and decent domestic happiness since they are despised by their wives. We also see that their constant preoccupation with the heavens has made them neglect their life on earth. Instead of aiming to live as well as they can, as men, they are in constant fear of astronomical **catastrophes** which are largely the fabrications of their ingenious intellects.

The flying island of Laputa is the seat of government for Balnibarbi the continent below. During Gulliver's first few days on Laputa, the island is flying toward the great metropolis of Lagado situated, of course, in Balnibarbi. Gulliver will have more to say about Lagado in Chapter IV below; however, at present, Gulliver is most concerned with fully exploring the curiosities of Laputa itself.

CHAPTER III

Gulliver receives permission from the King to investigate the curiosities of Laputa, particularly, the means by which the island navigates in the sky. He learns that the island is perfectly circular with a diameter of 7837 yards and, thus, an area of about ten thousand acres. Laputa is three hundred yards thick, top to bottom, and the lower surface of the island is an even, smooth plate of adamant (an archaic word for a material of impenetrable hardness.) This layer of adamant accounts for two hundred of the island's three hundred yards of thickness.

At the center of the upper surface of the island, there is a chasm about fifty yards in diameter at the bottom of which is a large dome known as Flandona Gagnole or the Astronomer's Cave. This place contains a great number of astronomical instruments but, most important, here is housed the mechanism which controls the movement of the flying island. This mechanism is a magnet of enormous size mounted on an axle which is part of the adamantine base of the island. The magnet consists of an attracting pole and, at the other end, a repelling pole. It is so mounted that either end can be made to point towards the island of Balnibarbi below; the magnet can also be made to rest in an oblique and a horizontal position. If, upon the King's command, the magnet should be positioned with its attracting pole pointed towards the island below, the flying island will then descend; on the other hand, if the repelling pole points toward Balnibarbi, then Laputa will rise directly upwards. With the magnet held in an oblique position, the island will rise or descend in a lateral direction and it is by maneuvering the magnet into several successive oblique positions that the astronomers are able to navigate, driving the flying island in whatever direction the King may demand. Should the magnet rest in a horizontal position, the island will remain stationary. Swift employs a mock diagram along with a **parody** (hilarious in its seriousness) of scientific and mathematical explanations to describe the motion of the island. In fact, it is generally thought that Gulliver's account of the island of Laputa is a **parody** of the reports of the Royal Society, that famous body of Englishmen devoted to scientific inquiry into almost everything.

The astronomers who look after the enormous magnet spend the greatest part of their time in observing and studying the heavenly bodies. For their studies, they possess telescopes far more powerful than those of Europe but much more compact in size. With their fine instruments, the Laputians have been able to catalog over ten thousand stars or three times as many as had been observed by European astronomers. They have also discovered two moons revolving about the planet Mars and ninety-three different comets.

Comment

It is not difficult to detect Swift's derisive tone behind Gulliver's account of all these astronomical achievements. We are asked to evaluate the importance of the celestial discoveries of the Laputians and we find that observing the heavens does not guarantee the good life on earth. The Laputians are fine astronomers but their wives are anxious to leave them forever.

Gulliver points out that the King of Laputa could exercise an almost absolute power over his subjects in Balnibarbi below. For, if a town below should engage in rebellion, the King has two methods of dealing with the situation and enforcing obedience. First, the milder alternative is to keep the island hovering over a town and its surrounding land, thus depriving the populace of sun and rain and inflicting crop failure and disease upon the land. If this method does not succeed in winning obedience from a recalcitrant people, the king proceeds to put into effect his second alternative; he lets the island drop directly upon the rebels, thus causing a universal destruction of houses and men. It is needed rare that the king resorts to this method; for one thing, his ministers can hardly approve of it except in the most serious situations because it would result in great damage to their own property all of which is in the land of Balnibarbi ... the flying island belonging entirely to the king. However, an even weightier reason for refraining from dropping the island on the heads of the rebels is that great damage could be done to the flying island in the process. Thus, it is the opposition of the King's ministers and the King's own fear of damaging his island that manage to prevent that monarch from exercising a potentially absolute and tyrannous power.

Comment

Most commentators agree that, in this account of the power politics involved in the relationship between Laputa and Balnibarbi, Swift is referring to the contemporary relations between England and Ireland. Obviously, it is in England's power to reduce Ireland to virtual slavery if England were to impose the full force of its economic and military might and, in the early eighteenth century, the history of Anglo-Irish relations amounts to the history of many such attempts. England, however, like Laputa, is not able to impose its will indiscriminately upon the weaker nation. Swift is trying to show that only a governmental arrangement that provides for a balancing of various interests (as, for example, those of the ministers of Laputa against those of the King) can provide safeguards against tyranny. Furthermore, Swift shows that the attempt to impose absolute subjection upon a part of a kingdom ultimately results in great danger to the aggressor. Thus, the Laputian King is reluctant to drop his island on the heads of his subjects below for fear of damage to his own domain.

CHAPTER IV

Gulliver soon begins to grow weary of his stay on Laputa. He is treated very well there but the King, and many of the people, treat him with a noticeable degree of disdain since he is far inferior to them in mathematics and music. On the other hand, he, for his own part, is rather bored with them; so wrapped up are they in their speculations that the only people he can speak to are women, flappers and tradesmen. This renders him all the more contemptible in the eyes of the Laputian intellectuals.

There is, however, one great lord with whom Gulliver is on good terms. This lord, a kinsman of the King, is not distinguished for his mathematical and musical attainments and is held in low esteem by the court. He is, however, most interested in what Gulliver has to say about Europe and often visits our friend and inquiries into the affairs of Europe, the laws, customs, manners and learning of that remote continent. This nobleman is distinguished by the fact that he needs no flappers; he merely keeps them about him for ceremonial purposes.

Comment

Here, Swift is contrasting the enlightened curiosity of a truly well educated man with the futile intellectual pursuits of the rest of the Laputians. Gulliver's friend is interested in essential knowledge. He wishes to know about the ways men live, the kind of knowledge that can be of practical help to him in managing his own life but, in the mad world of Laputa, his desire for this worthwhile knowledge makes him the object of contempt among the astronomers.

Gulliver is granted permission to leave Laputa and to visit Balnibarbi. His friend, the nobleman, gives him a letter of introduction to a nobleman in Lagado and, on the 16th of February, Gulliver is let down from Laputa at a distance of about two miles from Lagado ... the great city of Balnibarbi. He goes directly to the home of Count Munodi, the man to whom his letter of introduction is addressed.

The next morning, Count Munodi takes Gulliver on a tour of Lagado and its environs. The city is half the size of London but the houses are very strangely built with most of them out of repair. The people walk quickly through the streets, looking wild and ragged. As he passes out of the town into the countryside, Gulliver notices many laborers in the fields and a fine, fertile soil but, to his astonishment, the crops are hardly to be seen. In short, Gulliver exclaims to himself that he "never knew a soil so unhappily cultivated, houses so ill contrived and so ruinous, or a people whose countenances and habit expressed so much misery and want."

Gulliver is clearly amazed at these conditions. However, as his journey with Count Munodi continues and the two men approach the estate of the Count, the scene begins to change. Farming on the Count's estate is in a flourishing condition. The vineyards, wheat fields and grazing land are lovely to behold in their plenty. As Gulliver approaches the great house of Count Munodi, he sees that it is indeed "a noble structure, built according to the best rules of ancient architecture. The fountains, gardens, walks, avenues and groves were all disposed with exact judgment and taste." Gulliver is mystified. Why does this oasis of classical beauty, this estate so magnificently productive, stand out in such obvious contrast to the scenes of chaos and bareness to be encountered everywhere else in the neighborhood of Lagado?

Gulliver is even more mystified when Count Munodi tells him that, far from honoring him for his achievements on his estate, the governors of Lagado are convinced that Munodi is managing his affairs in a backward way and, therefore, are constantly harassing him into changing his manner of running his estate. In fact, Munodi realizes reluctantly that he will soon have to submit to increasing pressure to tear down his mansion and destroy his plantations in order to rebuild his home in the modern manner and to convert his farming methods to those approved officially. Gulliver is absolutely flabbergasted to hear this, especially after seeing how lopsided the buildings of Lagado were and how unproductive all the farms devoted to the new methods of agriculture were.

Munodi informs Gulliver that the source of all the trouble is the fact that many years before, on a visit to the flying island, some important citizens of Lagado became impressed by all the mathematical and astronomical learning in that unfortunate place. Upon returning to Lagado, they determined to reestablish everything … the arts, sciences, languages, agriculture … on a new basis. They set up an academy for this purpose, the Academy of Projectors. (A projector was a man who dabbled in projects, a sort of inventor.) This Academy would develop new schemes and new tools for accomplishing the tasks in any field of endeavor. The melancholy fact is, however, that not one of their schemes ever worked out well.

The agricultural and architectural mess that Gulliver observes everywhere around Lagado (except on Count Munodi's estate) can be blamed entirely on the ill-considered schemes of the Academy of Projectors yet, despite their failure, the Projectors exert great political influence and Munodi realizes that he, too, will soon have to submit to their pressure. In fact, he has already yielded to the Academy on a project for rebuilding a mill on his estate according to new principles. The old mill worked perfectly well and the new mill never worked at all but the projectors blame the project's failure on Munodi's lack of enthusiasm rather than on the shortcomings of their principles.

Comment

The reader will notice that Count Munodi's agricultural and architectural success is the direct result of his adhering to the traditional methods of farming and the fine architectural styles of the past. On the other hand, the Academy of Projectors advances many new and revolutionary schemes but these schemes are merely ingenious: they simply do not work. Now, Swift is not saying that everything that is new is bad merely because it is new; rather he is attacking a certain attitude that he feels was an unfortunate part of the new scientific spirit; the attitude that holds that anything that is new is good merely because it is new. What disturbs Swift most about his world is what appears to him to be its insane readiness to discard the wisdom of the past. Thus, what Swift is attacking, in the Academy of Projectors, is yet another manifestation of human pride: the idea that we can rely merely on our minds and native ingenuity in devising the manner of our lives. Swift would have thought that one of the chief touchstones of the life of an educated and humane man was his ability to make use of the best that the past achievements of the human race had to offer. The Projectors, however, are committed to novelty merely for the sake of novelty. Whether it is fair to equate the scientific spirit with that of the Projectors is another question. Undoubtedly, there is much that Swift does not understand about science; undoubtedly his attack is unfair because it is too sweeping but, on the other hand, many others who have misunderstood the scientific attitude have made the mistake of equating a scientist with a Projector. This is a mistake which any scientist would regard as deplorable.

CHAPTER V

Having heard so much about this mad Academy of Projectors. Gulliver is anxious to visit them to see their operations for himself. Thus, on his return to Lagado from the estate of Count Munodi, Gulliver is accompanied to the Academy by a friend of the Count. The Projectors, he finds, are not housed in a single building but in a conglomeration of buildings which have been wasting away. The Academy contains some five hundred rooms and each room houses at least one Projector.

The first man he meets is a meager fellow with sooty hands and face, long hair and beard, and a generally ragged appearance. For eight years, he has been working on a project to extract sunbeams from cucumbers. The extracted sunbeams are to be stored in hermetically sealed containers and are to be released on inclement summer days so that the air may be warmed. The Projector hopes to complete his project in another eight years and he begs Gulliver for some money to help his experiment along.

As he passes into the next chamber, Gulliver encounters a terrible stink; however, not wanting to give offense, he is good enough not to hold his nose. The man he now meets has the distinction of being the oldest Projector in the Academy and, in all his years there, he has been engaged in the same task: to convert human excrement back into the food from which it came. To make his experiments possible, the Academy sees to it that he is provided with a barrelful of human ordure per week. It is not surprising, therefore, that Gulliver is far from pleased when this Projector greets him with a hearty embrace.

In the next few chambers, Gulliver encounters a man trying to convert ice to gunpowder, an architect who devised a method for building houses from the top down (a method patterned on the practice of spiders and bees), and a blind inventor who, with the help of blind assistants, is trying (with no success) to perfect a method of mixing paints according to their feel and their smell.

One of the more interesting of the Projectors is one who is working on a new system of plowing; nuts and vegetables are buried in the ground and hogs are then let loose to hunt up the buried food. In the process of scrounging for the nuts and vegetables the hogs dig up the field, thus making it fit for sowing. The plan's only drawback is that the expense of the buried food is greater than the value of the crop to be planted.

The greatest Projector of them all, however, with some thirty years, experience in the business, is a most impressive man known to his colleagues as the universal artist. Currently, he is engaged in two great undertakings: the first is a project to discover a means of sowing land with chaff instead of seeds; the second is to find a means of preventing the growth of wool upon lambs. Ultimately, this Projector hoped to propagate a breed of naked sheep.

Comment

Swift adds very little to his depiction of the Projectors in the portraits mentioned above. In each case we see them engaged in projects which are laughably impractical or utterly useless. What, for example, would one do with a naked sheep, assuming that such an animal could be bred? Swift is making no attempt to supply the reader with a reasoned argument attacking science; he has chosen instead to exaggerate heavily, to write a burlesque on the scientific Projectors of his day in order to draw the reader's ridicule upon them.

After visiting the universal artist, Gulliver passes over into another part of the Academy of Projectors where the chief concern of the inventors is to find new methods of education and new approaches to the old subjects. For example, in one chamber stands a contrivance which contains every word of the Laputian language; a crank is connected to the contrivance and, when the crank is turned, the words are rearranged. Each time the words are rearranged, thirty-six boys peruse the contraption searching for three or four words that might have come together at random and that might form part of a sentence.

By filling up his notebooks with innumerable broken sentences, the inventor of this machine hopes eventually to create a body of arts and sciences, a collection of encyclopedic knowledge. Another project in the section of the Academy devoted to languages is an attempt to find a means of eliminating the need for language. Here, the Projector firmly believe that it is unhealthy to talk since every uttered word involves the destruction of an infinitesimal section of the lungs. The Projectors engage in research on this problem reason that words are only the names of things; if we, therefore, carry around with us those things about which we commonly talk, we could communicate without words; all we would need do is gesticulate while we held objects of our discourse in our hands. However, this innovation did not meet with the approval of the greater part of the population of Lagado. Most of the wiser men, nevertheless, are seen carrying enormous bundles of objects about with them; they use these in their mute conversations.

In the school of mathematics, another ingenious Projector has devised a new method of teaching young boys their geometry. The proposition and demonstration to be learned are written upon a wafer with a special ink. The student is made to swallow this wafer and eat nothing else for three days but bread and water. As the wafer becomes digested, the ink rises up to the boy's brain carrying the lesson along with it. However, for some unaccountable reason, the boys find this a most disagreeable method of learning geometry. It meets with the same failure any of the Projects in the Academy encounters.

Comment

Here, Swift is attacking not any specific educational proposal but rather, a general attitude towards education which views learning as a kind of mechanical process with certain clearly defined utilitarian aims. Thus, the man who would teach geometry through wafers is equivalent to a man who mistakenly sees the purpose of geometry to be the learning of propositions rather than the training of the mind. The point about these Laputian teaching machines is that they attempt to fill heads but they circumvent the process of study. A filled head, however, is not an educated mind; the former is fine equipment for a Projector, the latter is necessary for life. As for the proposal to eliminate language, it is easy to see that the loss of language would mean the loss of culture; the Projectors in this case are obviously unaware of the purposes language serves.

CHAPTER VI

Gulliver next visits the part of the Academy dealing with political Projectors; here are people whose sole employ is to think up schemes for running a government and it is here that Gulliver comes across some of the most outlandish schemes he has yet encountered; for example, some of these Projectors actually propose that Kings choose their favorites and award offices on the basis of the wisdom and virtue of the aspirants. They propose further that ministers be taught to consult the public good and that princes realize that their interest is identical with that of the people.

Comment

The reader may notice a slip in Swift's satiric technique here. These proposals of the political Projectors are eminently sensible; the only reason for considering them outlandish is that the world is corrupt. However, all through Book III, Swift has been depicting the Projectors as essentially ridiculous. Thus, it is inconsistent with his satiric technique to show these political projectors to be on the sensible side of things.

If we are surprised by these sensible Projectors, however, we soon enough encounter a number of their foolish colleagues; for example, one among them draws the common analogy between the body politic and the human frame. He extends his reasoning one step further and concludes that the state is to be treated, for its ailments, in much the same way that a man is treated for his. Thus, when the parliament of a nation convenes, this Projector proposes that the members be subjected to intensive physical examinations followed by the dispensing of medicines for the discovered ailments of the parliamentarians. In this way, the Projector hopes to achieve good government and a tranquil body politic.

Another Projector has devised a means of dealing with the short memories of royal ministers; those men who make promises and seem to forget to keep them. Any person having business with one of these ministers is to kick, pinch or tweak him by the nose; in this fashion the man's recollection of his promise will be reinforced. The petitioner is to repeat this treatment every time he meets the king's minister until the minister's commitment to the petitioner is fulfilled.

As a means of insuring that a senator's vote will be in the public interest, this same Projector suggests that each senator deliver his opinion on any measure up for a vote; after making his opinion clear, the senator is to be forced to cast his vote against his own position. In this way, we can be sure that his vote is in the public interest.

As a means of arriving at peaceful and moderate compromises on hotly disputed issues, this ingenious Projector suggests that the disputants be divided into groups of two according to the size of their heads; then, an operation is to be performed in which the brain of each man is divided in two, one half of each man's brain is exchanged for the corresponding half of his opponent's brain. Thus, with the "two half brains being left to debate the matter between themselves within the space of one skull, (they) would soon come to a good understanding." In this way, much public violence and factional dispute might be avoided.

Gulliver encounters a lively debate between two Projectors on the problem of devising the most efficient method of tax collection. One of them holds the opinion that a great deal of money could be collected if man's favorite vices and greatest follies were taxed. The other Projector, evidently convinced that man houses more pride than vice, firmly advocated that taxes should be levied on those qualities of body and mind for which men chiefly value themselves. Each man is to set his own tax relating it proportionately to his self-esteem. This, the Projector thought, is a surefire means of raising great revenues. Under this system of taxation, women are to be assessed according to their own estimation of their beauty and skill in dressing. Those who deem themselves most beautiful and most fashionable are to pay the highest taxes. The Projector is certain that the women will be only too happy to pay.

There is one area, however, in which Gulliver (because of his familiarity with English government) is able to make some suggestions which win the admiration of even the Projectors. Gulliver's suggestion concerns a technique for carrying on court intrigues, particularly, those intrigues designed to frame an innocent courtier by convincing the King that the said courtier is plotting against His Majesty. The Projectors express admiration at the ingenuity with which an intriguer in Gulliver's land is able to distort the perfectly innocent words and deeds of a completely innocent man in order to represent those words and deeds as proof of that man's treason against the king. The Projectors are truly impressed at the ease with which this method is able to ruin a good man's career and, while we laugh at the absurdity of the intriguers' misrepresentations, we are, at the same time, struck by the apparent frequency of such evil intriguing amongst the King's courtiers in England. We are suddenly reminded of the corrupt and secret plotting so characteristic of the court of Lilliput.

Comment

While Swift's depiction of the political Projectors is not great **satire**, it is based upon some interesting ideas which we have encountered before in the Travels. The political Projectors are not scientists but Swift depicts in them what one might call the scientific approach to government, or government by experts. Each of the Projectors has a "gimmick" which he believes will lead to some kind of improvement. These "gimmicks" all have the same fault in common: each is essentially a mechanical solution to a moral problem. Thus, one man holds that medicine administered to senators will automatically convert those senators into good legislators. Also, implicit in the approach of the Projectors, is the idea that the problems of government are of such a specialized nature that only specialized experts (the Projectors) can deal with them. Swift could not have disagreed more profoundly with this assumption. As we have seen in Brobdingnag, good government proceeds from good men; there is no special art involved and Lilliput proves that bad government proceeds from the deeds of bad, prideful men. Thus, the Projectors, in advancing "gimmicky," mechanical solutions to moral problems (the problems of good government), are misdirecting their efforts. Good government, Swift says, comes, not from good gimmicks, but only from good men.

CHAPTER VII

Having satisfied his curiosity concerning the Academy of Projectors, Gulliver is prepared to leave Lagado and return to Europe. He intends to make the return voyage by way of the islands of Luggnagg and Japan. Therefore, he sets out for the Laputian seaport of Maldonada hoping to catch a boat there for the island of Luggnagg. Arriving at Maldonada without incident, he is disappointed to discover that he will have to wait for some time for a boat headed for Luggnagg. He consequently agrees to a suggestion that he visit the tiny island of Glubbdubdrib, only five leagues off the Laputian coast. He makes the short journey in the company of two Laputian acquaintances.

The word Glubbdubdrib signifies "The Island of Sorcerers or Magicians." The governor of the island is the head of a tribe of magicians who preserve the purity of their calling by marrying only amongst themselves. The governor resides in a noble palace set in the midst of a grand park of some three thousand acres, all enclosed by a stone wall twenty feet high. The most remarkable thing about the governor and his family of magicians is the strange kind of domestic servants attending them.

Gulliver, to his horror and astonishment, discovers that the servants of the governor are the spirits of the dead who are at the call of the magician; he can command the service of any spirit for twenty four hours but he may not call on the same spirit more than once every three months.

Gulliver soon grows accustomed to having his food served by ghosts and responds with enthusiasm to the governor's offer to summon up from the dead any spirit with whom Gulliver might be interested in conversing. The governor tells his guest that he can ask the spirits any questions she might wish to and be assured of receiving truthful answers since "lying was a talent of no use in the lower world."

Gulliver's first impulse is to be entertained with scenes of pomp and magnificence; therefore, he has the governor summon the shades of the two great military heroes of the classical past, Alexander and Hannibal. The meeting, however, is a distinct disappointment for Gulliver. Alexander merely informs Gulliver that he died not at the hand of a treacherous poisoner but merely from a fever caused by excessive drinking. Hannibal is an even less impressive figure; this hero, whose mighty ambition it was to subdue Rome, finds nothing to tell his avid listener except that there was a complete lack of vinegar in his army's supplies. Gulliver then asks to see Caesar and Pompey at the head of their respective troops immediately before they engaged each other in battle. He asks the magician to call forth Caesar and Brutus and is quickly taken with a profound veneration at the very sight of Brutus. Gulliver sees in Brutus' face the signs of "the most consummate virtue, the greatest intrepidity, and firmness of mind, the truest love of his country, and general benevolence for mankind." Gulliver is pleased to discover that Caesar and Brutus were on good terms with one another; indeed, Caesar praises Brutus for the latter's patriotic and liberal motives in plotting Caesar's assassination. Gulliver learns that Brutus is often to be found in the company of Junius, Socrates, Epaminondas, Cato the Younger and Sir Thomas More; the six comprising a group unsurpassed for virtue and patriotism.

For his further edification, Gulliver asks the magician to summon for him the spirits of the senate of Rome, seated in one chamber; for comparison, he also asks that a modern parliamentary body be brought together before him. To his dismay, he discovers that, compared to the Roman senate which seemed to be composed of heroes and demi-gods, the modern assembly seemed to be as "knot of pedlars, pickpockets, highwaymen and bullies."

Comment

To the men of the early eighteenth century, the great figures of the classical past were looked upon with veneration as models of personal and political virtue. Swift (and Englishmen of his generation) turned especially to Augustan Rome, finding in that civilization an important analog to the experiences of England in the early eighteenth century. While Brutus was not a man of the Augustan period in Roman history, he is represented to us here as the very model of personal virtue and political responsibility. Brutus, it will be recalled, participated in the assassination of his friend Caesar out of his concern for the preservation of the

Roman republic. Swift here shows us that Caesar himself has come to honor Brutus for the action he was impelled to take against the dictator, an action motivated completely by the man's concern for his country. As opposed to this true patriotic and honest man, Swift shows us that the traditional figures of military glory and personal ambition (Alexander and Hannibal), are indeed sorry figures. Thus, Gulliver's conversation with the spirits in Glubbdubdrib is not merely a sensational ghost story; rather, it is still another vehicle for one of Swift's chief concerns in *Gulliver's Travels:* the delineation of the relationship between personal and political virtue, the good man and the good state.

CHAPTER VIII

Not wishing to miss the opportunity to converse with those of the ancients who were renowned for wit and learning, Gulliver sets aside one day on Glubbdubdrib for the purpose of conversing with Homer and Aristotle who are considered the greatest poet and greatest philosopher of all time. Homer is the taller and comelier of the two and he impresses Gulliver as having the quickest, most piercing pair of eyes our friend has ever beheld. Aristotle, on the other hand, is stooped, uses a cane, has a drawn face and hollow voice. Along with Homer and Aristotle appear the legions of critics and commentators who have, in the course of time, "so horribly misrepresented the meaning of those authors to posterity." Homer and Aristotle indicate, in no uncertain terms, that these critics and commentators are dunderheads.

Gulliver arranges a meeting between Aristotle and two famous modern scientists: Descartes and Gassendi. In the course of their conversation, Aristotle admits to the mistakes in his science of the natural world but he also explores the theories of Descartes and Gassendi. Furthermore, he predicts that the currently popular explanation of the natural phenomena, Newton's theory of gravity, will also be disproved in time. Aristotle maintains that "new systems of nature were but new fashions, which would vary in every age."

Having satisfied his curiosity for information about the ancient world, Gulliver turns his attention to the modern. A great admirer of the royalty and nobility of Europe, he is curious to see the ancestry of these great families. He is shocked and disappointed at what he encounters; far from being a group of noble figures, the ancestors of Europe's royalty merely make clear to Gulliver the sources of the defects of the so-called great families of his day. He discovers that the lineage of many as noble family is replete with "pages, lackeys, valets, coachmen, gamesters, fiddlers, players, captains and pickpockets."

Comment

Swift felt that one of the important constituents of a good society was an enlightened and public-spirited aristocracy, an hereditary aristocracy. He was, therefore, greatly disturbed by the fact that any man with enough money could purchase for himself a title in England and thus be raised to the nobility. In Swift's view, the landed, hereditary aristocracy was supposed to function as a kind of check to the power of the commercial classes; the middle class. Obviously, if the middle class could buy its way into the nobility the system would be upset; there would be no effective check against the power of money. It is this situation that Swift is attacking here in his unflattering depiction of the ancestry of the so-called aristocracy.

As he meets more and more of the spirits of the leading figures in modern history, Gulliver grows progressively more disgusted and disheartened with the modern world. Contrary to what he has read in history books, Gulliver discovers the true causes of many great events that have surprised the world. He finds that a whore in the person of a great man's mistress can exert great influence and virtually govern a kingdom; a general, renowned for bravery, confesses that he won a great victory purely by accidents which made his cowardice seem to be bravery; an admiral admits that he defeated, because of mistaken intelligence, an enemy to whom he had intended to betray his fleet; and three kings admit to Gulliver that they never advanced a person of merit unless it was by mistake. When he inquires of the possessors of great fortunes how they achieved their wealth and position, he is shocked to discover that they owed their power to the prostituting of their own wives and daughters, or to the betrayal of their country or their prince, or to poisoning, or to the perversion of justice and the destruction of the innocent. On the other hand, when he seeks to inquire about those who were virtuous (who had done some genuine service to their king or nation), Gulliver finds that these rare individuals are lost to history; having died anonymous, unrewarded and unrecognized for their services. Those honest men whose names are remembered have had their memories despoiled because the only reward for their decency was to be branded as traitors and rogues; such is the way of the world.

Gulliver finds, upon examining the spirits of the men of the modern world, that along with their moral decay is a corresponding physical deterioration, largely due to the spread of the pox (syphilis) among Europeans. Thus, Chapter VIII ends with an almost totally dispiriting view of the contemporary world; it is a scene of moral, political and physical decay.

CHAPTER IX

After experiencing this vision of modern decay, Gulliver takes his leave of the governor of Glubbdubdrib and returns to the Balnibarbian city of Maldonada. After two weeks of waiting, Gulliver finds a ship that is about to sail for Luggnagg and he boards it. The voyage from Balnibarbi to Luggnagg takes about a month during which time the ship encounters one violent storm but manages to arrive at Luggnagg without incident. On April 21, 1708, Gulliver's ship reaches the seaport town of Clumegnig and Gulliver disembarks.

Word gets out that Gulliver is a foreigner; he is told that it will be necessary for him to stay in Clumegnig for a fortnight, or until instructions come from the court concerning him. Because he wishes to go to Japan after seeing Luggnagg, Gulliver disguises the fact that he is an Englishman. He tells the Luggnaggians that he is a Dutchman; it will be remembered that Dutchmen (alone of all the natives of Europe) are permitted to enter the kingdom of Japan.

In order to facilitate his conversations with the Luggnaggians, Gulliver employs a young man, a native of Luggnagg who spent a number of years in Balnibarbi. This young man serves as Gulliver's interpreter.

As expected, in two weeks' time, word comes from the court directing that Gulliver be permitted to visit the great city of Traldragdubh (also pronounced Trildrogdrib). Gulliver arrives in that town and is given an appointment to meet the

Luggnaggian king. In order to conform to the custom of the country, Gulliver, upon his admittance into the royal presence, prostrates himself at the entrance to the King's chamber and crawls upon his belly towards the King, all the time licking the floor as he advances across the room. Because Gulliver is a stranger, the King directs that the floor be swept clean so that the dust should not prove annoying to the foreigner, who is unused to this strange custom. Gulliver tells us, however, that this is unusually considerate of the King, it being his practice to cover the floor with dust purposely on occasions when he wished to chastise his visitors. Gulliver himself, in his short stay at Luggnagg, sees "a great Lord with his mouth so crammed, that when he had crept to the proper distance from the throne, he was not able to speak a word." This is an especially disconcerting position for a man to get into because to spit or wipe one's mouth in the presence of the King is, in that country, a crime punishable by death. Furthermore, concerning capital crimes, the Luggnaggians devised an ingenious method of execution; the condemned man is forced to lick a floor upon which a brown powder (a deadly poison) has been spread. The King is careful, however, to have the floor washed immediately after such an execution. In this way he shows his concern for the lives of his innocent subjects, only a few of whom have accidentally met their deaths by innocently licking a poisoned floor not intended for them.

When Gulliver, creeping towards the King, reaches a spot four yards from the throne, he strikes his forehead gently against the ground four times, as he has been instructed to do, and says the following words, also as instructed: Ickpling gloffthrobb squutserumm blhiop mlashnalt zwim tnodbalkguffh slhiophad gurdlubh asht. This is the compliment established by law which all persons admitted to the King's presence must deliver to the King. The English translation is approximately as follows: "May your celestial Majesty outlive the sun, eleven moons and a half."

The formalities out of the way, the King and Gulliver settle down to some interesting chats. The King is delighted with Gulliver's company and Gulliver is rather pleased with the King who made several offers of his hospitality should Gulliver decide to stay on in Luggnagg for life. Gulliver, however, is determined to return home to his wife.

CHAPTER X

Despite their peculiarly Oriental pride (an example of which we have seen in the previous chapter in the King's attitude towards his subjects), the Luggnaggians prove to be a surprisingly congenial people. They behave courteously to Gulliver and he makes many interesting acquaintances. It is in the course of a conversation with some of his Luggnaggian friends that Gulliver comes to learn of the remarkable struldbruggs, or immortals, a truly unique feature of Luggnaggian life. When he expresses wonder at the use of the term "immortal" to describe human creatures. Gulliver is told that, on extremely rare occasions, a child is born with a red mark on his forehead, directly over the left eyebrow. As the child grows, the spot becomes larger and changes color; at twelve years it is green, at twenty-five, blue, and, at forty-five, black. After this, the spot remains unchanged. The people who are distinguished in this peculiar fashion have the further and most remarkable peculiarity of possessing eternal life!

Imagine Gulliver's reaction to this discovery! Overwhelmed with delight at the idea of a people who live forever, free of that continual apprehension of death which is so heavy a weight on the human spirit, Gulliver becomes rhapsodic as he expresses his wonder at the very thought of the struldbruggs. In response to a question put to him by his Luggnaggian friends, Gulliver relates in enraptured words exactly what he would do and how he would manage his life had he the great good fortune of enjoying eternal life. He would spend the first two hundred years of his life gathering riches in order to free himself for higher pursuits in the course of eternity. Thus, after becoming the wealthiest man in the Kingdom, he would devote himself to becoming the most learned. He would then use his wisdom in forming and directing the minds of young people so that they could become useful and virtuous citizens. He would surround himself with the company of the wisest and best of the struldbruggs, a company surely unsurpassed for wisdom born of experience. He would watch the course of human history unfold before his undying scrutiny; he would thrill to new discoveries and be witness to the perfecting of great inventions. Eternal life, in short, is a prospect of infinite joy to Gulliver.

How surprised he is, therefore, when he discovers that his Luggnaggian friends are listening to him with wry smiles on their faces, obviously amused at what must be the misguided thoughts of their foreign friend. They rudely remind him, furthermore, that everything he has just said is based on the assumption that eternal life implies eternal youth, health and vigor. However, no assumption could be faultier! Indeed. Were he to see some of the struldbruggs, he would quickly conclude that death is a blessing rather than a curse. Gulliver is treated to a description of the life of a struldbrugg.

Up to the age of thirty, these unfortunate immortals (he is told) lead a life which is much like that of common mortals but, beyond that age, they grow progressively more melancholy and dejected until they reach the age of about eighty. The struldbruggs decline into age and decrepitude at the same rate as all mortals do and, thus, when they reach the age of eighty, they have all the infirmities of old age but their plight is made all the more miserable by the fact that they can look forward only to eternal decay, unrelieved by the blessed release of death. Because of this, they are a rather peevish group: tormented by envy and the frustration born of desires they are incapable of satisfying. Their envy is directed on the one hand at the pleasures of youth which they are eternally witnessing and eternally prevented from enjoying, and, on the other hand, at the deaths of the old, deaths which the struldbruggs see as an eternal rest which they themselves never can hope to have.

At the age of eighty struldbruggs are declared legally dead: their heirs immediately inherit their estates: they are permitted no important employment: they cannot purchase land or take part in any way in civil or criminal trials. At ninety, physical decay is most debilitating. The unfortunate immortals lose their teeth and hair and sense of taste: thus, they are unable to take pleasure even in their food. They remain subject to disease and their memory, even of those persons nearest to them, is entirely lost. In this way, they are deprived even of the pleasure of reading, since their minds cannot bring them from the beginning to the end of a sentence without their forgetting what they have read.

Such is the account given to Gulliver of the miserable struldbruggs, miserable because they are doomed to immortality. He is later to meet five or six of these poor beings, the youngest of whom is not above two hundred years. Although they are told that Gulliver is a traveler from a faraway land, they show no curiosity towards him at all but merely ask him for slumskudask; that is, alms. To Gulliver, the struldbruggs are the most horrible sight he has ever seen; in addition to the physical decay one would expect to find in extreme old age, these poor creatures acquire an indescribable ghastliness in proportion to their years. So terrible is the appearance of these beings that Gulliver makes no attempt to depict it.

His meeting with the struldbruggs is sufficient to convince Gulliver of the foolishness of his first response to his discovery of their existence. He regrets that he cannot bring a specimen of these beings back to England with him as an object lesson on the foolishness of the fear of death.

| Comment

Swift, in his brilliant depiction of the struldbruggs, is commenting upon one of the more pervasive human vanities, the wish to escape death. Swift is showing us that, in failing to come to terms with death, we fail to incorporate into our lives what is perhaps the most important condition of life, that it must, at some point, end. Swift shows, with much poignant sympathy, that it is precisely our knowledge that life and pleasure are not eternal which makes our lives and pleasures precious. To hope for eternal life, therefore, is to blind oneself to the realities of human existence and, consequently, to deprive oneself, of whatever possibility there is to find happiness in the only life one has. To fear death is to be blind to one's human limitations. The desire for eternal life is thus another species of human pride, the essential sin of man and the central **theme** of *Gulliver's Travels*. The reader should recognize, however, that, in depriving us of the illusion of immortality, Swift is not "pessimistic." Quite the contrary, for, if we are aware of our limitations, then we are aware of our capabilities, and the purpose of Swift, in this book, is to make us aware of our human capabilities.

CHAPTER XI

On the 6th of May, 1709. Gulliver takes his leave of the King of Luggnagg and bids farewell to all of his Luggnaggian friends. The King is sincere in his efforts to convince Gulliver to stay on in Luggnagg but, seeing that his guest is determined to return home. His Majesty bids him a gracious farewell and provides him with a letter of introduction to the King of Japan. As parting gifts, the King gives Gulliver four hundred forty-four large pieces of gold and a red diamond which Gulliver is able to sell in England for eleven hundred pounds.

Gulliver sails from the Luggnaggian port of Glanguenstald, on the southwest of the island. After a voyage of fifteen days, he arrives at a small port in Japan called Xamoschi. When he shows the Japanese customs officials his letter from the King of Luggnagg, Gulliver is greeted with great dignity and provided with a conveyance to the great city of Yedo where he has an audience with the Emperor.

Gulliver continues his pretense of being a Dutch merchant and begs two favors from the Emperor which His Majesty graciously grants out of deference to Luggnagg's king who has given Gulliver so fine a letter of introduction to the Japanese prince. The first is to give Gulliver safe passage to Nangasac ... from whence the traveler may sail home to Europe. The second (and by no means easily granted) favor is to exempt Gulliver from the requirement of trampling on the crucifix; a practice to which all Dutchmen are subjected in Japan. The Emperor is rather surprised to see that Gulliver has scruples in regard to the cross and mentions to Gulliver that he is the first Dutchman the Emperor has met who has shown any reluctance to partake in this ceremony which is so disrespectful to the Christian religion. He warns Gulliver further that although he, the Emperor, is willing to exempt his guest from trampling on the crucifix, the other Dutchmen would not take the matter as lightly and might even attempt to murder Gulliver if they discovered that he did not trample on the sign of their faith. In fact, to dispel any objections the Dutch sailors might raise, the Emperor makes it seem that Gulliver's failure to trample on the cross is the result of an official oversight rather than an official favor.

Comment

Swift is making a jibe here at the Dutch who were probably better merchants than they were Christians. He depicts them as all too willing to comply with the Japanese demand that they trample on their cross in return for the privilege of trading with those Oriental islands. Indeed, Swift shows the Dutch in a particularly bad light: they are even more thoroughgoing than the Japanese require them to be in their observance of this sacrilegious custom.

Gulliver arrives at Nangasac on June 9, 1709 and, soon after that, sails for Europe on a Dutch ship, the Amboyna, commanded by one Theodorus Vangrult. The captain agrees to transport Gulliver at half rate in return for his services as ship's surgeon. Throughout the homeward voyage Gulliver carefully continues to pretend that he is a Dutchman.

On April 16, 1710 the ship arrives in Amsterdam and, four days later, Gulliver finds himself back in England. He goes straight to his home in Redriff where he rejoins his family after an absence of exactly five years and six months.

ANALYSIS OF BOOK III

Considered in terms of its satiric technique, Book III is probably the least satisfactory section of Swift's great work. In Books I and II, Gulliver is presented as a figure of interest in his own right and the reader's relationship to Gulliver is carefully manipulated by Swift in order to evoke, in the reader, a dramatic response to the incidents and experiences of the book. Thus, in Book I, we identify with Gulliver and feel ourselves morally superior to the tiny, cruel and prideful Lilliputians. In Book II, on the other hand, we alternately identify with Gulliver and with the Brobdingnagians; at one moment, we see ourselves in Gulliver's shoes and sympathize with the (now) little man who struggles so valiantly (and foolishly) to preserve his dignity against the threats posed against it by the mighty giants; at another moment, we tend to identify with the giants. We find ourselves looking at Gulliver through Brobdingnagian eyes and discovering that he is, indeed, a despicable little creature.

In Book III, however, there is not much interest developed in Gulliver as a character; he is, rather, a mouthpiece for the opinions of Swift. Gulliver's responses to the world of Laputa, to the Academy of Projectors and to Count Munodi are not really his own reactions but that of his creator. The one exception to this is seen in Gulliver's encounter with the struldbruggs; this is generally considered to be the best part of Book III.

The modern reader finds it hard to sympathize with the attack on science and technology as it is developed in Book III. However, if we consider Swift's position here in the context of the great and pervasive **theme** of the book as a whole, we can evaluate at least the reasons why a great mind distrusted science. To Swift, the scientific approach to experience was another species of that great and basic human sin of pride, in this case, an overwhelming pride in the capacity of the human intellect to deal with human problems. Thus, in the Academy of Projectors, all sorts of projects are devised; but, they are devised by men who approach their problems only with thought. Now thought, by itself, may be ingenious, but it is also impractical. It is ingenious to try to extract sunbeams from cucumbers, to build houses from the top down, to exchange the brains of ideological opponents; but, ingenuity is not enough in human life. Therefore, Swift asks us to contrast the impractical, almost insane schemes of the projectors with the common sense of Count Munodi whose mansion is beautiful and whose fields are fruitful. Count Munodi relies not only on intellect but, also, upon traditional wisdom in his search for solutions to human problems. His house, for example, employs the best styles of the past and is a lovely building while the rest of the buildings and farms around Lagado are ugly ruins or barren lands. Count Munodi relies not merely on his own intellect but, also, upon the best that past human experience has to offer. He recognizes the limitations of intellect (and is therefore free of pride) while the scientists and projectors, unaware of the limits of the human mind, are the victims of pride. Furthermore, as we saw in Lilliput, the victims of pride always defeat themselves; the Lilliputians are forced to expel from their midst a man, Gulliver, who could have been of enormous help to them. The Laputians lead a miserable life; the schemes of the projectors never work. This is Swift's logic; this is the essence of his attack on science and technology in Book III. The scientists and projectors lead a crazy life because they are blind to their limitations as human beings. The great purpose of *Gulliver's Travels* is to delineate the nature of the good life, the life based upon knowledge of man's capabilities. However, in order to show man exactly what his capabilities are, Swift chooses to make man aware of his limitations. In Book III, he depicts the limitations of the human intellect by burlesquing and ridiculing science and technology, two fields which, Swift thought, were based upon a dangerously erroneous conception of the infinite ability of the human mind to handle all human problems.

GULLIVER'S TRAVELS

TEXTUAL ANALYSIS

BOOK IV

....

| INTRODUCTORY NOTE

While Gulliver has learned much about human folly and vice in the first three books, he has remained a great believer in mankind. His adventures have been eye-openers but they have not turned him against man. The reader will remember, however, that the man we met, writing about himself in his letter to the publisher at the very beginning of this book, was mad with the madness of misanthropy. In Book IV, we discover how Gulliver's journey into a discovery of what man is becomes a journey into madness. We encounter, here, a cruel attack on man. This is an attack utilizing two of the most striking literary **metaphors** for man: the Houyhnhnms and the Yahoos. The first are beings in every way like horses except for their possession of absolute reason; the second are creatures bearing an uncanny resemblance to man except for their animalistic brutality. Swift's use of these creatures, Houyhnhnms and Yahoos, as an approach to the problem of the nature of man, has attracted more critical attention than has any other part of his work. As we move into Book IV, we shall see why for the Houyhnhnms and Yahoos are going to provide Gulliver with the most crucial and devastating experiences of his life.

CHAPTER I

After becoming reunited with his family, Gulliver remains at home this time for only five months. He now accepts an offer to take part in another voyage, as captain of the merchant ship Adventure, and sets sails on September 7, 1710, leaving behind his wife who is pregnant.

It is an ill-fated voyage. Before long, many of Gulliver's men fall sick and die; it becomes necessary for him to recruit more sailors which he does when his ship reaches the Barbados and the Leeward Islands. Unhappily, the new recruits have many former pirates among them and, in a short while, these criminals succeed in corrupting the rest of the crew. The pirates lead a conspiracy to wrest control of the ship from Gulliver and the plot is quite successful. At the threat of immediate death should he refuse to submit, Gulliver surrenders to his captors who chain him to his cabin. A guard is posted at his door with orders to kill Gulliver on the spot should he try to escape.

On May 9, 1711, Gulliver is told by one of the seamen, James Welch, that the new captain has decreed that Gulliver be set ashore and abandoned. This desperate measure is immediately carried out and Gulliver is left on the shore of an unknown island with no weapon but his short sword and no possessions but his clothes, some trinkets and a little money. Gulliver gathers together his trinkets; he intends to present them to the first savage he may meet hoping, thereby, to purchase his life. He resolutely begins his trek into the interior of the island and is somewhat pleased to see that it is not a savage wilderness. There is plenty of grass, long rows of trees, and several fields of oats.

As he continues his exploration, Gulliver happens upon a beaten path with many tracks of human feet and horses' hooves. Finally, he comes upon several animals in a field; these beasts are unusually shaped and apparently deformed; their heads and breasts are covered with hair; they have goat-like beards and a ridge of hair down their backs and on the foreparts of their legs and feet. Otherwise, their bodies are bare with skin of a brown buff color. They have no tails and often are found sitting on the ground on their buttocks. Often, they stand about on their hind legs and they are able to scamper up high trees with the nimbleness of squirrels because of their strong and extended claws which grip the sides of the trees. Gulliver views these creatures with disgust and remarks that he never beheld in all his travels so disagreeable an animal, "or one against which I naturally conceived so strong an antipathy."

Comment

The animal which arouses so much disgust in Gulliver is, of course (in its physical respects) a particularly bestial version of the human physique. At this point, in his first encounter with the beasts (later, we discover that they are called "Yahoos") Gulliver is so repulsed by them that he fails to recognize in them any resemblance whatsoever to human beings; soon, however, he will make the cruel discovery of this resemblance with unfortunate results for himself.

As Gulliver continues along the road, one of these odious creatures jumps in his way, blocking his path. Not wishing to do him much harm, Gulliver strikes the beast with the flat part of his sword whereupon the animal draws back and howls as loudly as he can. Soon, Gulliver is surrounded by a pack of these ugly beasts, all howling and making odious faces but not attacking him. Some of the beasts, however, clamber up a tree and, from its branches, they discharge their excrement on Gulliver.

Suddenly, in an instant, the creatures disperse, running away from Gulliver. He cannot account for the cause of their sudden fear; but, as he turns around, he notices a horse walking softly in the field at the side of the road. The horse is momentarily startled at the sight of Gulliver but he regains his composure and approaches the man, looking him directly in the eyes. The horse examines Gulliver's hands and feet carefully but, when Gulliver's attempts to stroke the animal's neck, the horse removes Gulliver's hand with his left forefoot and neighs three or four times. The animal does this in so remarkable a manner that, to Gulliver, it seems as if the horse has a language of his own.

Another horse soon comes up to join the first. They seem to greet each other in a formal manner; touching their right hooves together and neighing in turn. Again, Gulliver is struck with the quality of their neighing which seems to be that of articulate conversation. The two horses walk a few paces away from Gulliver and confer together about this strange new creature ... a man ... within their midst. Gulliver is quite happy to see so much reasonable behavior in the animals of the island; if the horses are so "civilized" then what magnificent men must inhabit this place!

The two horses approach Gulliver once more and examine him very carefully. They fondle his clothes not realizing that these are clothes but, rather, thinking that they are part of Gulliver's body. In examining Gulliver's right hand, one horse unintentionally squeezes it tightly between his hood and pastern; causing Gulliver to roar with pain. After this incident, the horses use all possible tenderness when examining the stranger. Particularly perplexing to these apparently rational creatures is Gulliver's footwear. Not understanding the use of stockings and shoes, the horses are at a loss to account for what seems to them a most inefficient foot structure.

So impressed is he with the rational behavior of these animals that Gulliver decides that they must be human beings changed, by a magician, into the shape of horses. Thus, he decides to speak to them. He delivers an address, begging them to lead him to a house or village, telling them of his misfortunes on sea, and offering, in return for their help, those several gifts he has about him. However, if Gulliver was amazed at the behavior of the horses, they in turn are astonished when they see that this figure in their midst is capable of speech. They again confer between themselves, this time, obviously engaged in serious conversation. Gulliver is able to distinguish, because of their frequent reoccurrence, two words in the speech of the horses, the words yahoo and houyhnhnm (pronounced winim). When Gulliver repeats these words aloud, the horses realize that they have some sort of prodigy in their midst. The two horses take leave of each other and one of them, the grey, indicates to Gulliver that he should walk in front of him. When Gulliver, somewhat weary, tries to slacken his pace, the horse cries hhuun, hhuun urging the man forward. However, when he understands that Gulliver is tired, he permits the man to rest. In this manner, the strange procession of man and horse continues on its way, towards what Gulliver hopes will be some human habitation.

Comment

Here, in the first chapter of Gulliver's final adventure, Swift skillfully sets up the terms within which that adventure will take place. We have creatures whose behavior is absolutely bestial but whose shapes are human. These are the yahoos, although, at this point, we have not yet been told that this is their name. On the other hand, we have creatures whose behavior is in every way rational but whose shape is that of a beast, a horse. Gulliver is caught between these two beings and soon discovers just to what extent he shares the characteristics of Yahoo and Houyhnhnm. Swift, however, has forced this discovery to come about in a rather cruel manner. By giving the horses reason, he has so arranged the terms of Book IV that Gulliver will be forced to look at himself and his England through the eyes of these horses: that is, he will be forced to see himself in a most harshly objective light. His physical and moral characteristics will be examined as objectively as we examine a horse's coat or a sheep's wool. This is the effect of Swift's approach in Book IV; it will have the consequence of leading Gulliver into madness.

CHAPTER II

Having covered about three miles in their walk, Gulliver and his guide, the horse, come to a long building made of timber with a low roof covered with straw. Comforted at the thought that he is finally about to meet the man who owns these marvelous horses, Gulliver takes from his pocket those trinkets which he hopes will buy decent treatment. The grey horse beckons Gulliver to enter the buildings; he does so and comes upon a large room with a smooth clay floor. A rack and manger extend along the length of one side of this room. The remarkable thing about this room is that there are three horses, two of them mares, quietly engaged in domestic business! Upon orders from the grey horse, the others let Gulliver pass without molesting him. Apparently, the grey holds a position of some authority over the other animals.

Beyond this first room there are three others which comprise the entire length of the house. As Gulliver and his guide approach the last room, Gulliver surely expects to meet the man who is master of the house and he notices that the horse is somewhat ceremonious as he announces his presence to the occupant of this last room. Stopping to take stock of these fantastic events, Gulliver begins to think that he must be dreaming. Surely, this island must be under the spell of some magician if the men in it are served by horses, and horses who can reason …! but, of course, there are no human masters on this island. For when Gulliver enters the next room, the last, where he had expected to meet the man who was master of all these animals, his sight is greeted by more horses, a mare and her colt, sitting on their haunches upon mats of straw which are carefully made and perfectly clean and neat. Gulliver now begins to understand that these horses themselves are, in fact, the lords, masters and governors of the country!

Soon after Gulliver enters this last room, the mare rises from her mat and comes up close to the stranger. She observes his hands and face very carefully and, having completed her examination, she gives Gulliver a most contemptuous look. She steps aside and confers with the grey horse. Throughout their conversation, Gulliver again hears the word yahoo repeated with great frequency; he still does not know what that word means but he will soon find out. The grey, beckoning to Gulliver with his head, leads the man out of the house into another building nearby. Here, Gulliver sees three of those odious creatures he had encountered earlier. They are feeding upon roots and the flesh of asses and dogs. The creatures are tied by the neck with strong rope which is fastened to a beam. Holding their food between the claws of their forefeet, they tear at it with their teeth.

The grey horse, evidently the master, orders a sorrel nag (one of his servants) to untie one of the ugly brutes and take it into the yard. Here, Gulliver is brought close to the beast and the faces and bodies of the beasts and the man are carefully compared. To his mortification, it now begins to dawn on Gulliver that the abominable animal being held near him possesses an exact resemblance to the human figure and face in almost every way. True, the face is flat and broad and, perhaps, the creature is far uglier than the average Englishman but, without any doubt, this odious beast possesses a human form. All this while, Gulliver hears the word yahoo repeated again and again by the horses who are standing by. It is now clear to him that the beasts are called yahoos and that the horses are quite aware of the fact that Gulliver is very much like the Yahoos in appearance.

Comment

It is an understandably great shock to Gulliver to discover that he, a man and an Englishman, bears a closer resemblance to the Yahoos than to the rational life on the island, the horses. We will observe now that he makes every attempt to dissociate himself from the Yahoos, to hide (from the horses) his physical resemblance to the beasts.

The Houyhnhnms, struck by the resemblance Gulliver bears to the odious Yahoos, are nevertheless mystified by Gulliver's clothes which they continue to believe are part of the man's body. Gulliver is pleased to let them continue thinking so because he would like the horses to believe that he is a representative of a species quite distinct from the odious Yahoos.

The horses test for further resemblances between their new guest and the Yahoos; they offer Gulliver several samples of Yahoo food: roots, asses' flesh, etc. Gulliver, however, declines their offers. He also declines to share in the diet of the Houyhnhnms which, as we might have guessed, consists largely of oats and hay. In fact, Gulliver's diet presents quite a problem since he realizes that he cannot be nourished by the food of the horses nor by the food of the Yahoos. Temporarily, he satisfies his hunger by drinking milk, which is plentiful, but it takes some ingenuity on his part before he manages to devise some solid nourishment. This he does by calling for some oats which are brought to him by one of the servants Houyhnhnms. Gulliver warms the oats and separates the grain from the husks. He then grinds the grain between two stones, adds water and, thus, makes a kind of paste which he forms into the shape of a flat cake. He bakes this dough at the fire; making a kind of bread which he eats warm with milk. Although, at first, this diet seems rather tasteless to him, Gulliver slowly grows accustomed to it, supplementing it occasionally with a rabbit and herbs which he boils and eats as vegetables. He grows accustomed quickly to the lack of salt in his diet. All in all, he is quite impressed to discover how little is required to satisfy our natural necessities.

Comment

We can see Gulliver slowly becoming accustomed to a new kind of life, the life of reason which he is forced to imitate from the model supplied by the horses. We can begin to see that Gulliver is impressed by the orderly and rational conduct of life he sees in the Houyhnhnms but, while the Houyhnhnms may provide Gulliver with a model manner of life, Swift is forcing the careful reader to judge whether the life of the horses is indeed a proper model for the life of man. It may be true that a man can subsist on a diet of oats and milk and even thrive on them; but, are oats the only alternative to asses' flesh, the food of the Yahoos? In other words, Gulliver's choice of diet is not really the point; rather, his choice of diet signifies his choice of a manner of living as we shall see. Swift is now asking us to consider whether Gulliver is making a proper Hhoice. We may say that the rest of Book IV is an answer to that question.

The master horse (that is, the grey who had been Gulliver's guide) provides his new guest with a place to stay, some six yards from the main house and separated from the stable of the Yahoos. Gulliver makes a bed from some straw, covers himself with his clothes, and is able to sleep very soundly.

CHAPTER III

Now, Gulliver customarily refers to the grey horse as his master and, under his master's tutelage Gulliver sets about learning the Houyhnhnm language, a project to which every member of the Houyhnhnm household contributes. Gulliver writes down in a notebook the names of things and studies his notes when he is alone. A sorrel nag, one of the master's servants, helps Gulliver with his pronunciation. Gulliver remarks that the language of the horses closely resembles in its pronunciation, the high Dutch or German language.

The master is most impatient for Gulliver to learn the language so that he may be questioned concerning his origin and former life. Also, the master continues to be somewhat at a loss to understand what kind of creature Gulliver is: the man is so like a Yahoo and, yet, is distinguished from those odious beasts by his teachableness, civility and cleanliness. These are qualities directly opposed to those of the Yahoos and, of course, the fact that Gulliver is capable of speech and language is an indication that, unlike the Yahoos, he possesses some quantity of reason. It is this which most mystifies the master Houyhnhnm: he is most curious to learn how it came about that a creature like Gulliver, resembling so closely the most unteachable of brutes, learned how to imitate a rational creature.

Comment

To the horse, it is inconceivable that Gulliver can possess the gift of reason; at most, the horse is willing to admit that Gulliver has learned somehow to imitate a rational creature. The horse's attitude, of course, represents a threat to Gulliver's conception of himself since he is subtly forced into seeing himself through Houyhnhnm eyes. The effect of this, as we shall see, is to cause Gulliver to lose sight of the fact that he is neither Houyhnhnm nor Yahoo, but is a man: after all, he is teachable, civil, and clean. The Yahoos are not.

In about ten weeks, Gulliver has made enough progress with the language to understand most of his master's questions. In three months, he is able to supply tolerable answers. The master is most anxious to discover where Gulliver came from. When he is told that Gulliver came in a ship across the sea and was abandoned by his mutinous crew, the horse has considerable difficulty understanding Gulliver. In the first place, the master is convinced that Gulliver is saying the thing which is not (the Houyhnhnm expression for a lie) because the master knows that there can be no country beyond the sea.

Furthermore, even if there were, it is inconceivable to him that so marvelous a thing as a ship could be maneuvered (let alone built) by Yahoo brutes: why, this is even beyond the ken of Houyhnhnms!

Comment

So perfect is Houyhnhnm life that their language possesses no word for the idea of "falsehood." To tell lies is inconceivable to them. However, if they possess perfect reason, Swift is also showing us that perfect reason itself has its limitations. The Houyhnhnms, for example, are positive that their island is the universe and they simply cannot conceive of the possibility that a Yahoo-like creature may not be a full-fledged Yahoo.

The report of a strange new creature (a Yahoo with glimmerings of reason) begins to spread to the master's neighbor Houyhnhnms who come frequently to visit Gulliver and speak with him. They are most amazed at the peculiar covering on his body (his clothes) and doubt that he can be a regular yahoo. Gulliver, of course, is happy to let them continue believing this.

However, one night, while Gulliver is asleep, the sorrel nag enters his quarters on orders from the master. It is Gulliver's habit to strip himself and cover himself with his clothes when he sleeps, but it happens that his improvised blanket has slipped off him in the course of the night. Thus, the sorrel is quite surprised when he sees the naked Gulliver and he runs off in a fright to tell his master of the amazing change in Gulliver's body.

It is now clear to Gulliver that he must tell the master the secret of his clothes. This he does, explaining in some detail the use of clothes and demonstrating by stripping himself naked in front of the master who examines Gulliver's body very carefully. The master now sees very plainly that, except for considerable differences in the quantity of body hair and in the smoothness of their skins, Gulliver and the Yahoos are identical creatures.

Gulliver is mortified and begs the master not to use the term Yahoo in reference to him; he requests further that the master keep secret (and command the sorrel not to divulge) the truth about his body and its resemblance to that of a Yahoo. The master agrees.

Comment

This is a crucial point in the book for, at this moment, Gulliver is taken with a loathing of his own body. He is making the mistake of viewing himself through the eyes of the Houyhnhnms and seeing, not merely a resemblance between himself and the Yahoos, but an identity. He is thus in the process of developing a contempt for himself, a contempt based upon a standard of perfection (the Houyhnhnms) which is not meant for him. This self-contempt is the first step in the onset of the madness which is now inevitable.

Gulliver holds many conversations with his master in which they discuss Gulliver's native country. It is with great difficulty that Gulliver explains to his skeptical master that, in England, it is the Yahoos who have the reason and the Houyhnhnms who are the brutes. It is especially hard for the master Houyhnhnm to believe that Yahoos like Gulliver can perform so marvelous a task as navigating a ship across the ocean.

CHAPTER IV

The master Houyhnhnm is most uneasy as he continues to listen to Gulliver's account of a world in which reasonable behavior is to be encountered in Yahoos. The horse is uneasy because it is difficult for him to give credence to Gulliver's tales. And since it is so rare for a Houyhnhnm to find himself in the act of doubting (or not believing) he is somewhat at a loss in dealing with Gulliver's apparently outlandish account of life beyond the borders of Houyhnhnmland. Indeed, so honest are the Houyhnhnms with each other that their language does not even contain a word for lying. Thus, when the master hears a story that seems as fantastic as Gulliver's he simply does not know how to respond. He feels that Gulliver must be saying the thing which is not.

What is absolutely inconceivable to the master Houyhnhnm is that Yahoos are the governors of Gulliver's homeland while Houyhnhnms are only the servants. Gulliver tries to placate his master's growing indignation by explaining to him how well the English Yahoos care for their Houyhnhnms; or horses, as they are called in England. However, when Gulliver balances his account honestly by telling his master of the uses to which most English horses are put and of the cruel way they are treated when they pass into old age, the master Houyhnhnm becomes most resentful. He expresses his resentment in his refusal to believe that a Yahoo-like creature can really be the master of a horse, let alone a nation! In support of this opinion, the master Houyhnhnm tries to show Gulliver that, even should he possess some glimmer of reason, his Yahoo-like body is contrived too poorly to use that reason in the common affairs of life, in fact, Gulliver's physical equipment is even inferior to that of a common yahoo. For example, his nails serve no purpose; his forefeet (the

Houyhnhnm's name for Gulliver's hands) are too soft to be used for walking, while, on the other hand, his habit of walking only on his two hind feet is impractical since he can easily fall. Gulliver's head and face, furthermore, are impractically formed since his nose protrudes and his eyes are too close together. Gulliver's body contains, in itself, no protection against heat and cold but is, in fact, so inefficient that it must be covered with the skins of other brutes. Then, in addition to all of these shortcomings, the very ugliness of the Yahoo frame causes all other creatures naturally to abhor the Yahoo thus making it impossible for the Yahoos to tame other animals to their service. Such, at least, are the speculations of the master Houyhnhnm concerning the impossibility of a Yahoo-like creature ever performing the tasks of a rational being. Rather than continue with idle speculations, however, the Houyhnhnm invites Gulliver to explain further, if he can, in exactly what manner life is conducted in Yahoo society in England. The Houyhnhnm is particularly interested in Gulliver's account of his own life.

Comment

Here, the master Houyhnhnm is forcing Gulliver to examine himself through Houyhnhnm eyes. Obviously, the effect of such an examination is to arouse shame in Gulliver for his own body. This, of course, is a mistake on Gulliver's part for, as a man, he is not meant to view himself in the cruelly objective light of a Houyhnhnm's vision. Under the continuing assaults of the Houyhnhnms, Gulliver will see more and more of the Yahoo in himself; but he is, after all, not a Yahoo. He is a man. It is this fact that he begins to overlook; but he overlooks it because he is compelled to view himself through the eyes of the only other rational creatures on the island, the Houyhnhnms.

With some difficulty, Gulliver tries to explain to his master the circumstances of his last voyage. Especially difficult for the master horse to understand are the reasons why Gulliver was able to recruit a crew after so many of his men had died. Gulliver tries to explain to the master that men hounded by poverty or hunted as criminals will take any measure that makes it possible for them to flee their country: but the master is rather obtuse here. He cannot understand why a man should practice the vices and excesses that must lead him into poverty or crime. Gulliver tries to give the master an account of how men are goaded by lust, intemperance, malice and envy into a life of excess and crime but, for the Houyhnhnm who is free from these impulses, it is only with great difficulty that he comes to understand something of human nature as it manifests itself in Europe.

Comment

While it is obvious that the Houyhnhnms are some sort of ideal figures, the reader should note that it would be a mistake to take them as valid models for human imitation. They may be better than humans but it must be remembered that they are different from Humans. Houyhnhnm life is much simpler than human life because these ideal horses are not possessed of the impulse towards evil that is so powerfully present in many. Man's life is a good deal more difficult; he can be good, but with great effort, while the Houyhnhnms are good without effort and are consequently not nearly so interesting as men are. Gulliver's great mistake is his blindness to the poignant difficulty involved in man's attempts to battle his baser instincts in order to lead the good life. Gulliver will be blinded by the glorious but inhuman example of the Houyhnhnms.

CHAPTER V

As Gulliver slowly settles into life in Houyhnhnmland, he has many conversations with the master Houyhnhnm concerning English life. In this chapter, he informs us of the master's observations on two of England's more prominent preoccupations: war and law.

    Gulliver gives the master an account of the war that England has been engaged in with France, the war over the Spanish succession. When he is told that some million Yahoos (as Gulliver now calls his fellow humans) lost their lives in this war, the master expresses some curiosity about the causes that goad men into such massive self-destruction. Gulliver tells him that frequent causes of war are ambition, corruption, greed and pride. By far the most common cause of war, though, is difference in opinions; furthermore, the more trivial the disputed opinions are, the more bloody and cruel is the war which settles the issue. Thus, European yahoos are often found killing each other over questions of religious doctrine: "whether bread be flesh or flesh be bread; whether the juice of a certain berry be blood or wine; whether whistling be a vice or a virtue; what is the best color for a coat, whether black, white, red or grey, etc."

Comment

Swift's approach here is quite subtle. We must never forget that Gulliver is now observing English life through the eyes of the Houyhnhnms. Therefore, his account of the differences in religious opinion among Europeans naturally makes those differences seem inconsequential, if not silly, but, what is silly to the Houyhnhnms is not necessarily silly to men who are, after all, not impossibly perfect creatures. On the other hand, while religious differences are important to men, it is despicable that they should murder each other over these differences. In other words, we can gain some significant insights into our faults by viewing them through Houyhnhnm eyes. The total objectivity of the Houyhnhnm view, however, is proper only to Houyhnhnms and not to men. Thus, men might try to stop killing each other over their religious differences but they probably should not try to abandon those differences. Gulliver, however, in looking at human life with the unnatural objectivity of a Houyhnhnm, begins to despise not only the abuses of our beliefs but our beliefs themselves.

Gulliver goes on to describe, in greater detail, the innumerable reasons which men can find for slaughtering each other. The master is horrified to hear these things but he reflects that men are fortunate in not having the power to inflict on each other a torture proportionate to the hate they bear each other. He therefore indicates that Gulliver must be saying the thing which is not when he tells of how many millions of men are killed in wars. How tragically amusing it is to Gulliver to see such innocence in his noble master! How sad he is to tell his master of the ingenious ways men have found to circumvent their physical inefficiency in inflicting destruction upon one another! True, their claws (nails) are not good for fighting but they have guns, powder, swords, cannon, and so on. In short, it is easy for Gulliver to convince the master that men are quite efficient at killing each other and the master is disgusted to hear of human weapons. It is now clear to him that human beings are indeed worse than Yahoos. For humans have corrupted what little reason they possessed and, in its corrupt form, reason is worse than Yahoo brutality; it becomes an efficient instrument of cruelty.

Upset and disgusted by Gulliver's account of man and war, the master wishes to change the subject and inquire into the institution of law in England. He remembers that Gulliver's crew contained some men who were ruined by law and he wonders how it is possible that law could become a man's ruin when it was intended to do just the opposite (i.e., preserve man within society). Gulliver tries to explain that a lawyer's job is to prove "that white is black and black is white" depending upon who is paying the lawyer. Thus, if a man's neighbor should take a liking to that man's cow, a lawyer will easily be found who will be willing to argue, with great skill, that the cow belongs to the dishonest claimant. Only by hiring another lawyer can the honest man, at great expense, hope to retain possession of his own cow. Furthermore, the honest man can expect very little help from the judge since the judge himself is likely to have been a most dexterous lawyer in his youth.

Comment

Swift is attacking here the corrupt manipulation of law for dishonest purposes. He attacks the abuse of law on the part of lawyers and clients who have forgotten that the only purpose of law is to insure justice. Swift shows that an honest man, strangely enough, has most to lose in a society in which law itself is a tool of the corrupt. And he attacks those unscrupulous lawyers who place their reason at the service of injustice.

CHAPTER VI

Gulliver proceeds to depict, in greater detail, the manner of life in Europe but he has considerable difficulty explaining to the master Houyhnhnm the motives behind the behavior of the European Yahoos. The reason for his difficulty is that the master has no conception of the meaning or use of money, that strange thing that seems to be the cause of everything the Yahoos in Europe do. The Houyhnhnms have no conception of money because they have no use for it; things are so arranged in Houyhnhnmland that every Houyhnhnm has his share of the necessities of life. Therefore, when Gulliver tries to explain that, in England, poor men labor in order to provide luxuries for the enjoyment of the few who possess great amounts of money, the master is at a bit of a loss to understand. Gulliver explains, for example, that England is capable of producing enough food to feed its population three times over but, nevertheless, most Englishmen are on the verge of starvation because the food produced is shipped abroad in order to pay for the luxuries that a few can afford and for which most ruin themselves. The master is particularly perplexed to learn that the English import great quantities of drink. He cannot understand why this should be necessary when water is so plentiful. It is not water which is imported, but wine, "a sort of liquid which made us merry by putting us out of our senses, diverted all melancholy thoughts, begat wild extravagant imaginations in the brain and banished our fears." The master has no conception of the phenomenon of drunkenness nor of the "purpose" it serves.

Gulliver goes on to describe the diseases to which English Yahoos are susceptible, and their causes. He explains that the eating and drinking habits of an English Yahoo are not determined by the needs of his body but by his desire for delicacies and drunkenness. Englishmen ate "when we were not hungry and drank without the provocation of thirst: we sat whole nights drinking strong liquors without eating at bit, which disposed us to sloth, enflamed our bodies and precipitated or prevented digestion." He goes on to explain how venereal disease is destroying the health of his nation and how it is the result of a wanton sexual indulgence directly comparable to the gastronomical indulgence just described. The result of this way of life is that most Englishmen are physically decrepit, suffering from an innumerable variety of maladies. It is with great difficulty that Gulliver explains to the master the function of a physician and the contemporary state of medical practice. He ridicules the various theories the physicians hold concerning the origins and treatment of disease: he ridicules them because they look only for the merely physical cause and symptoms of human illness and do not recognize that physical illness is the direct result of moral weakness and therefore cannot be cured by purely physical treatment. In his description of contemporary medical practice. Swift is quite funny as he **burlesques** the ideas and methods of early eighteenth-century medicine.

The master is somewhat at a loss to understand all of his since illness is utterly unknown among the Houyhnhnms who suffer only on the occasion of accidents. They never get sick before they die; the only sign that death is approaching is a feeling of weakness that manifests itself a few days before the death of one of these perfect creatures.

Comment

One of the things that Swift feared was the effect of a growing money economy in England. As the society grew more and more wealthy, as England became more and more engaged in world commerce, the money that naturally accrued to a few was spent on what Swift called "luxury." It was not wealth but the poor uses to which wealth was put that he feared. Thus, he shows us here that the monied groups decay morally in their corrupting consumption of luxuries and, along with this moral decay, suffer from physical disease. The poor are not exempt for they too yearn for wealth and become criminals in order to obtain it. The Houyhnhnms, however (who live according to reason), seek only to satisfy their needs; consequently, there is no crime and no disease, no lawyers and no doctors in their island.

In the course of their conversations. Gulliver once mentioned to the master that government in England is headed by a First or Chief Minister of State. The master Houyhnhnm has no idea what a minister of state is, so Gulliver explains that he is a creature who "makes use of no other passions but a violent desire for wealth, power and titles." A first minister "never tells a truth but with an intent that you should take it for a lie, nor a lie, but with a design that you should take it for a truth." Furthermore, "those he speaks worst of behind their backs are in the surest way to preferment; and whenever he begins to praise you to others or to yourself, you are from that day forlorn. The worst mark you can receive is a promise, especially when it is confirmed by an oath, after which every wise man retires and gives over all hopes."

Comment

In this extremely unflattering depiction of a King's minister, Swift's specific target was probably Robert Walpole, the Whig Prime Minister whom Swift despised. However, Swift is attacking, in general, the hypocrisy and corruption which are at the basis of politics when politicians are not patriots but self-seekers. It is noteworthy that the Houyhnhnms have no conception of politics or first ministers since their gift of reason enables them to govern themselves; we have not yet been told exactly what kind of reason they possess but, at this point, we can see that all actions based upon Houyhnhnm reason are beneficial to individual Houyhnhnms and, at the same time, to the Houyhnhnm community. Thus, they have no need of politicians or of government.

The master Houyhnhnm pays Gulliver a huge compliment one day. Noting that Gulliver "Far exceeded in shape, color, and cleanliness all the Yahoos of [Houyhnhnmland] and ... was not only endowed with the faculty of speech but likewise with some rudiments of reason," the master concluded that Gulliver must have been an aristocrat in England. Gulliver thanks the master for his high opinion of him but explains honestly (and ironically) that, in England, the nobleman is distinguished not by his fine physical constitution but, rather, by disease and decrepitude brought on by habits of idleness and indulgence in "luxury." Furthermore, since a nobleman usually squanders his fortune on "luxury," he is forced to marry (merely for money) women who are old, ugly, sick and of mean birth. Consequently, the children of such marriages are unhealthy and many noble families are dying out.

CHAPTER VII

These conversations Gulliver held with his master (taking place over the course of two years) were eye-opening experiences for the Englishman. Forced to view his former life and native country through the superior moral vision of the Houyhnhnms, Gulliver becomes completely disgusted with the human race and, even before he has been in Houyhnhnmland for a year, he firmly resolves never to return home but to spend the remainder of his life with these noble horses. As we shall see later, he will not be permitted to do so.

One morning, after these conversations have been concluded and the Master's curiosity has been satisfied, he sends for Gulliver, and delivers his own judgments on human nature, judgments based on the information Gulliver has given him and on what he has observed in the Yahoos. He concludes that humans possess only some pittance of reason rather than the genuine reason of the Houyhnhnms; furthermore, they have used this pittance of reason not to better their conditions but to "aggravate [their] natural corruptions, and to acquire new ones which nature had not given [them]."

The master then goes on to describe some of the habits of the Yahoos and to compare these habits with their more sophisticated counterparts in Gulliver's Europe. It is obvious to the master that the institutions of government and law so unflatteringly described by Gulliver are necessary because of man's defects in reason; if man had sufficient reason, he could govern himself. To confirm this opinion, the master cites the example of the Yahoos. Yahoo life, like human life, is marked by constant dissension. It is this dissension which necessitates (in Europe) lawyers and a government. Now, if food enough for fifty Yahoos in Houyhnhnmland should be thrown to five of those odious creatures, rather than eat peaceably, the brutes will attack each other, each one trying to get all the food for himself. If a Houyhnhnm's cow should die, the Yahoos of several neighborhoods would fall into pitched battle over the animal's carcass and, on occasion, the Yahoos would fight with each other without any reason. In addition, if they could not arrange a fight with the Yahoos of a neighboring district, they would engage in a kind of civil war within their home district.

Further, after speaking to Gulliver, the master begins to understand another characteristic of the Yahoo breed, a peculiar trait which heretofore had been a mystery to him; that is, the beasts are unusually fond of stones of several colors and will spend days digging for these stones with their claws. Once, as an experiment, the master removes a heap of these stones from the kennel of a Yahoo who collects them. "Whereupon the sordid animal missing his treasure, by his loud lamenting brought the whole herd to place, there miserably howled, then fell to biting and tearing the rest: began to pine away, would neither eat nor sleep, nor work" until the stones were brought back to him. The Yahoos' attachment to these stones must be caused by that same vice which makes it impossible for them to share their food among themselves: avarice. Gulliver is able to see the human desire for money in its basic terms: as a kind of bestial impulse giving rise to vicious dissension among the Yahoos affected by it.

Paralleling the human tendency to eat and drink beyond the demands of nature, the Yahoos render themselves odious by their "appetite to devour everything that came in their way, whether herbs, roots, berries, corrupted flesh of animals, or all mingled together." They eat until are ready to burst. Especially pleasing to them is a root for which they fight bitterly because sucking on it seems to procure for them the same effects that wine produces in men as Gulliver has explained this to the master. "It would make them sometimes hug, and sometimes tear one another; they would howl and grin, and chatter, and roll, and tumble, and then fall asleep in the mud." It is not at all surprising, therefore, that the Yahoos are the only animals on Houyhnhnmland who are subject to disease, disease arising not from ill treatment but from their own-nastiness and greed. So free are the Houyhnhnms from disease that their language has no terms for the maladies of the Yahoos. In order to provide a name for these sicknesses, the Houyhnhnms link their word for evil with the word Yahoo and thus develop a term, hnea-yahoo, for the maladies of the brutes.

The master sees no immediate resemblances in Yahoo life to the institutions of government among the English but he does notice that there seems to be, in each Yahoo herd, a sort of head Yahoo: this beast is distinguished by being the most deformed and mischievous of his group. He is served by another Yahoo whose job it is to "lick his master's feet and posteriors, and drive the female Yahoos to his kennel for which he was now and then rewarded with a piece of ass's flesh." The master Houyhnhnm is not sure to what extent these customs of the Yahoos resemble the customs of the English court with its favorites and ministers of state.

Of all the qualities of the Yahoos, that which most distinguishes them from the other beasts is their disposition for nastiness and filth; the brutes are seemingly untouched by any impulse toward cleanliness. In defense of man, Gulliver realizes that, in Europe (at least), swine are filthier than men: but, since there are no swine in Houyhnhnmland, Gulliver does not try to explain this to his master.

Sometimes, a Yahoo mystifies the Houyhnhnms by taking himself into a corner: and, there, getting down and howling, groaning and complaining. The Houyhnhnms never discover the cause of this behavior but they are well aware of the cure: they merely take such a groaning Yahoo and put him to work after which he always comes to himself. Gulliver sees in this a parallel to those fits of depression which seize upon the "lazy, the luxurious and the rich, who, if they were forced to [work]" might be cured of their symptoms.

The Houyhnhnms also note that the female Yahoos are adept at the tricks of lewdness and coquetry which they use to attract the male beasts. Gulliver is astonished to see these civilized arts so firmly grounded in the savage instincts of the Yahoos.

| Comment

In Chapter VI, Gulliver describes for his master human avarice, gluttony, disease and political corruption. In this, Chapter VII, the Houyhnhnm master traces the original sources of these "civilized" vices back to the behavior of the bestial Yahoos. In the process, Gulliver is forced again to see human behavior mirrored in the lives of those disgusting brutes; that is, he is subjected to the shattering vision of man as an animal. It is an experience from which he does not recover but, as we shall see, he has not properly understood its meaning.

| CHAPTER VIII

Gulliver is now convinced that he can learn much about human nature by observing the Yahoos. Consequently, he asks and receives permission to go among them. He is careful, however, to arm himself with his short sword because the Yahoos have apparently sensed some resemblance to themselves in the figure of Gulliver and, on occasion, have approached him closely.

The Yahoos are very nimble creatures: they are excellent swimmers from infancy and often catch fish which they bring home to their young. They have a terrible odor about them; somewhat between the smell of a weasel and a fox. Out of curiosity, Gulliver catches a three year old Yahoo cub one day; the man tries to keep the little beast quiet by showing it some tenderness but so loudly does the brute wail that Gulliver is soon surrounded by a band of adult Yahoos. He has to let the little beast loose but the creature manages to squirt Gulliver's clothes full of excrement.

Gulliver observes the Yahoos to be virtually unteachable; the height of their capabilities seems to be in drawing burdens. However, Gulliver is convinced that they are unteachable not because they are stupid beasts but because they are nasty.

One day, Gulliver undergoes a mortifying experience. When he walks about in Houyhnhnmland, he is generally in the company of the sorrel nag, the servant Houyhnhnm whose job it was to guard Gulliver. But, on one hot day, Gulliver receives permission from the sorrel to take a swim in the nearby river. He strips naked and plunges into the water. Imagine, however, his disgust when he observes a young female Yahoo observing him from the bushes with a lascivious look in her eyes. The beast is not content with merely watching; inflamed with desire, she leaps into the water and embraces Gulliver. Never before has he been so terrified and so humiliated. Roaring as loudly as he can, he attracts the sorrel who comes to his rescue. The Yahoo lets go her grasp with utmost reluctance and runs howling to the opposite bank of the river where she watches Gulliver put on his clothes. Although the Houyhnhnms are amused by his occurrence, to Gulliver it is the most mortifying experience of his life.

Comment

None of Gulliver's experiences is as cruel as this one; he has, all along, been trying to maintain some kind of distinction between himself and the Yahoo but, when he is sexually assaulted by a female Yahoo, he himself takes the incident as proof of his essential identity with the beasts. He apparently overlooks the fact that, although the beast was attracted to him, he was not attracted to her.

Having supplied us with a fairly complete picture of the Yahoos, Gulliver now undertakes the difficult task of representing to us the life of these remarkable creatures, the Houyhnhnms. As we know by now, these marvelous creatures submit their lives to the rule of reason; but we do not know exactly what reason is as it is cultivated by these horses. Gulliver tries to explain. Reason, he tells us, as it is practiced by the Houyhnhnms is not a tool to be used for problem-solving. Perhaps that is what reason, in its corrupted form, means to humans but, when the Houyhnhnms exercise their faculty of reason, they see the truth immediately. There never is, among them, any question of a difference of opinion; humans, on the other hand, are capable of arguing both sides of a question when they exercise their reason. To the Houyhnhnm, however, there never are two sides of a question. Reason shows them the truth and, since all Houyhnhnms possess reason, all Houyhnhnms agree as to the nature of the truth. Perhaps a better word for the reason of the Houyhnhnms is "insight" or "intuition," but it is an intuition which is infallible. The eighteenth century man would have understood Houyhnhnm reason in terms of the ancient classical idea of "right reason" - an idea which became an important element in Christian thought.

Comment

It is now clear that the Houyhnhnms possess a kind of reason in which human beings simply do not and cannot share. Unlike Houyhnhnm reason, human reason is indeed fallible, as Swift has been at pains to show us throughout the book. It therefore follows that human beings cannot hope to become Houyhnhnms. They can, however, benefit by imitating certain Houyhnhnm ways but it is extremely important here that the reader notice that Houyhnhnm reason is a different thing from even the best developed human reason. It is immediate insight into truth. Human reason, on the other hand, is a tool we use to help us grope towards probabilities. Moreover, Houyhnhnm reason is not only insight into truth; it is insight plus an inevitable concomitant of right action on the part of its possessor.

The two principal virtues among the Houyhnhnms are friendship and benevolence; but, again, the Houyhnhnms cultivate a kind of friendship which seems strange to human beings; for a Houyhnhnm is as much of a friend to a remote stranger as he is to his nearest companions. Each Houyhnhnm is friendly in the same degree to all other Houyhnhnms. Furthermore, the horses (in a similar manner) make no distinction between their own colts and the offspring of a neighbor. As we might expect, Houyhnhnms do not marry for love but for procreation and, when a couple has produced one colt of each sex, they no longer have sexual relations with each other. It never occurs to a Houyhnhnm to commit adultery because reason tells him that procreation is the purpose of sexual relations.

The Houyhnhnms take great care to educate their young who are taught temperance, industry, exercise and cleanliness. The females are educated in the same way as are the males, it being a Houyhnhnm belief that one responsible for the upbringing of the young should be no mere domestic drudge. The Houyhnhnm young are trained in strength, speed and hardiness by running races. Four times a year, the colts of a district meet to show their proficiency in running and leaping and the victor is rewarded with a song made in his honor.

Should it happen that one Houyhnhnm family has two children of the same sex, the family merely exchange one of those children for one of the opposite sex from another family. Since no irrational attachments are formed between parent and colt, no tears are shed on such occasions. There is no reason for them since colts, like friends, are interchangeable in Houyhnhnmland.

Comment

After depicting for us the reason of the Houyhnhnms, Swift goes on to show us what kind of life follows from this kind of supreme reason. It is here that a complex response is evoked from the reader towards these marvelous horses. Certainly, their supreme sanity is attractive compared to the unreason that rules England and the bestiality of the Yahoos. However, the reader (unlike Gulliver) recognizes that human life is more difficult than Houyhnhnm life for the simple reason that the Houyhnhnms cannot make mistakes; they are automatically good, so to speak. The interest, pain, joy, glory and despair of human life, on the other hand, arise from the fact that man's will and reason often are in conflict and the proper resolution of this conflict is the drama of human life. A man must struggle to be good; a Houyhnhnm cannot help succeeding. Consequently, if Houyhnhnm life is better, human life is more exciting. Although the Houyhnhnms never grieve over their children or their friends, neither do they experience the joy which sometimes comes to a human as the result of his emotional attachment to another. Gulliver, however, has by now forgotten what it means to be human so dazzled is he by the reason of the horses and the bestiality of the Yahoos. The reader, however, is not asked to accept Gulliver's conclusions; he must evaluate them by mediating (as a man) between the virtues of the Houyhnhnms and the potential defects of men. For Gulliver, this has become impossible.

CHAPTER IX

Although the Houyhnhnms have no government, they do call meetings of a Representative Council every fourth year at the onset of the season of spring. At these meetings, they inquire into the state of the several districts of Houyhnhnmland to make certain that the necessities of life are in sufficient supply in each district. It is at these meetings, for example, that the supply of oats, hay and Yahoos is evenly distributed, the regulation of children is determined and the necessary exchanges are made. The Council also is prepared to debate any important issues that may arise but, in point of fact, the only topic that is ever debated (and it comes up at every meeting) concerns the Yahoos; whether that odious breed should be exterminated from the face of earth.

Those Houyhnhnms who argue the affirmative on this question point out that Yahoos did not always inhabit Houyhnhnmland. Tradition held that, many ages ago, two of the brutes appeared upon a mountain; their origin unknown. They reproduced and, in a short while, grew so numerous that they threatened to overrun the nation. It was necessary for the Houyhnhnms to declare a Yahoo hunt during which most of the beasts were killed; only enough were left alive so that each Houyhnhnm could keep two young ones in a kennel and train them for whatever work they could do. As time passed, the Yahoos tended to replace the asses as work animals and those Houyhnhnms who argue for the extermination of the brutes point out that except for their superior agility, the Yahoos are in every way inferior to the asses as beasts of burden. All things considered, these Houyhnhnms think, the Yahoos should be exterminated.

Gulliver's master comes up with an alternate plan, however. First, he remarks that the original two Yahoos were driven hither from across the sea and then abandoned by their companions. Subjected to life in a savage environment, they gradually degenerated into the brutes now inhabiting the land. The master offers Gulliver as living proof of this theory of the origin and decay of the Yahoos. The master then tells the Council of a procedure that the English Yahoos employ in taming horses in England and suggests that the same be done to the Yahoos in Houyhnhnmland: namely, castrating the young which would effectively put an end to the breed without actually destroying life. Gulliver, however, never discovers the decision at which this Council arrived regarding this matter.

Comment

In the master's account of the origin of the Yahoos, we see that the brutes do not represent human beings but what human beings must become when they are removed from civilization. However, lest we comfort ourselves with this thought, we must remember that Swift has also shown us that civilization, in itself, guarantees nothing. We must live not merely in society but in a good society.

Gulliver proceeds to supply us with some more details of Houyhnhnm life. Interestingly enough, these horses have no written literature of any kind. They have no use for it; being a perfect race, nothing of note ever happens to the Houyhnhnms. In effect, they have no history; for what is history, after all, but a record of war, death, inventions and conquests, none of which ever occur or are found in Houyhnhnmland. As opposed to the Laputans, the Houyhnhnms are most backward in their astronomy; they know enough to calculate the course of the year by the movement of the sun and the moon and they understand the causes of eclipses. Their poetry is excellent but it is not written. The most common subjects of Houyhnhnm poetry are friendship, benevolence and athletic honor.

A Houyhnhnm can expect to live to an age of about seventy or seventy-five years. The only cause of death is old age (except for occasional accidents) and, since reason tells them that death is the natural and inevitable end of life, they feel neither joy nor grief at their departure from this world. Gulliver is quite amazed, one afternoon, when the wife of one of the master's friends is late for a visit; she excuses herself by explaining that her husband died that very morning and she was necessarily detained by the funeral arrangements. Her behavior during the visit is quite as cheerful as that of anyone present.

The Houyhnhnms are never taken by surprise by death; they can tell about ten days before they die that the end is near and they use the time to visit all of their friends. The Houyhnhnm word for death is lhnuwnh which means to retire to the first mother.

Comment

Some critics point out that the Houyhnhnms' attitude toward death is remarkably similar to that of the Stoics. We know that Swift scorned stoicism as a meaningful guide to human life; consequently, these critics argue that Swift is actually attacking the Houyhnhnms (whom he presents as symbols of extreme rationalism) and, perhaps (through the Houyhnhnms) he is satirizing those rationalists of his day, the Deists. Other critics deny this. In any event, whether he is attacking the Houyhnhnms or not, it is clear that their attitudes towards life and death cannot be those of a human being. We may derive some benefits from imitating certain of their ways but we cannot become like them. If we try to, we go mad as does Gulliver.

CHAPTER X

As time passes, Gulliver grows more and more accustomed to living in Houyhnhnmland. Indeed, never before in his life has he known the peace and contentment he discovers here. He inhabits a little room which was built for him about six yards from the home of the Houyhnhnms; he is able to sew new clothes when his old ones wear out, and he fashions, for himself, outfits made from Yahoo skin. He devises traps made of Yahoos' hair in which he catches an occasional rabbit which serves him as a rare delicacy. Indeed, he is self-sufficient and well provided for, having learned how easily nature is satisfied, and nothing makes him happier than his realization that he is far removed from the vices of English life. "I had no occasion of bribing, flattering or pimping, to procure the favor of any great man, or of his minion. I wanted no fence against fraud or oppression: Here was neither physician to destroy my body, nor lawyer to ruin my fortune, no informer to watch my words and actions, or forge accusations against me for hire."

One of Gulliver's chief delights is to sit in on the visits paid to the master by the neighbor Houyhnhnms. Gulliver never speaks unless he is asked to and rather prefers to keep quiet so that he may benefit from the precious talk of the Houyhnhnms. Indeed, never before has he heard anything paralleling the magnificence of their conversation, conversation marked by the most exalted notions on the most important subjects. So much does Gulliver venerate these marvelous horses that he can no longer bear to look at the reflection of his own face; without quite realizing it, he begins to imitate the speech of the horses and their manner of walking. To this day, he tells us, he often falls into the voice and manner of the Houyhnhnms.

Comment

If we consider the picture of a man walking and talking like a horse, we can understand Gulliver's description of himself here;

he is, at this point, clearly mad. His madness will be strikingly obvious when we see him, in the next chapter, establishing his first human contact since landing on Houyhnhnmland.

Dazzled by the life of the Houyhnhnms, imitating that life as best he can, Gulliver clearly is incapable of returning to human society. Yet, the cruelest day in his life now dawns upon him for the master informs him of the shocking news that the Assembly of Houyhnhnms has decided that Gulliver must be put off the island! The Houyhnhnms can see only potential danger in the presence of Gulliver and will not even consider permitting him to remain on the island in the capacity of a regular Yahoo. It is not out of compassion for Gulliver that the horses wish to prevent him from living with the Yahoos; rather, it is their fear that he may, with his glimmer of reason, make evil use of the brutes against the Houyhnhnms that convinces them that he must be sent away.

Gulliver falls in a faint upon hearing this news. When he comes to his senses, he utters a lamentation. He tells his master how much he would have preferred death to banishment; how dreadful, far more dreadful than death, is the prospect of returning to live among the English Yahoos; how difficult it would be for him to build a little boat for himself since many of the necessary materials are not to be found in Houyhnhnmland. However, Gulliver makes no attempt to persuade the Houyhnhnms to change their minds since he knows that, among them, the dictates of reason are not to be questioned. The master listens to Gulliver courteously and gives him two months in which to build a ship with the help of the sorrel nag.

The first thing Gulliver does is to survey the sea around Houynhnmland; he discovers an island lying in the distance, to the northeast of the land of the horses. This island, he resolves, will be his first destination.

With a destination in mind, he sets about building his ship and, in six weeks' time, he constructs a sort of Indian canoe whose covering is made of Yahoo skins. He loads the canoe with a supply of boiled rabbit flesh, a vessel filled with milk, and another with water.

When the time comes for his departure, Gulliver bids a tearful goodbye to his master and the whole Houyhnhnm family. The master does Gulliver the honor of lifting his hoof so that Gulliver may kiss it without prostrating himself on the ground. Gulliver then steps into his canoe and pushes off, beginning the journey that will take him back to his own kind.

Comment

Swift has so arranged this poignant chapter that we cannot help but sympathize with Gulliver and censure the Houyhnhnms for their unfeeling treatment of him. True, the dictates of reason prompt them to remove from their midst this potential source of corruption, but this only points up the limitations of reason alone as a guide to human life. The Houyhnhnms seem unaware of the emotional effect of their purely rational decision on Gulliver but Swift, of course, has the last laugh for he has caused us to sympathize with Gulliver. And yet, we must remember that Gulliver is miserable exactly because he is forced to come back to us!

CHAPTER XI

It was on February 15, 1714-5 at nine in the morning, that Gulliver sailed away from Houyhnhnmland. The master and his friends stayed on the shore until Gulliver was out of sight and, often, the poor exile heard the sorrel nag (who had become attached to Gulliver) crying out Hnuy illa nyha maiah Yahoo. Take care of thyself, gentle Yahoo.

The banished man's intention was to discover some small uninhabited island which could furnish him with the necessities of life and on which he could pass the remainder of his days away from humanity. Searching his memory, he recalls that his ship was in the vicinity of the Cape of Good Hope when his crew mutinied and abandoned him. Thus, he steers his ship in a direction which he hopes will bring him to New Holland; near New Holland he hopes to find the island haven.

On the afternoon of the second day of his journeying, Gulliver arrives at the southeast coast of New Holland. He remains on the shore trying to keep his presence hidden from the natives. For three days, he lives on oysters and raw shellfish but, on the fourth day, he ventures a bit too far inland; he is spotted by a group of natives, stark naked savages. They immediately chase Gulliver and wound him seriously with an arrow in his left knee but he is able to reach his canoe and paddle himself out to sea at a safe distance from the savages.

As he looks around for another haven, Gulliver suddenly spies a sail in the distance. He debates with himself whether to wait for the ship to reach him and rescue him or to turn back to the place from which he has just run. So horrible to him is the prospect of returning to live in England among Yahoos that he decides to return to the savages and hope for the best among them. However, he is thwarted in this because he is discovered by the sailors of the ship when they stop at the island for water.

When the seamen speak to Gulliver, he is horrified, so unused is he to the sound of human speech. Furthermore, when he answers them in his now strange tone of a neighing horse, and, in addition, tells them strange stories of Houyhnhnms and Yahoos, the sailors are convinced that he is a madman. Nevertheless, they treat him kindly and, at the captain's orders, bring him aboard ship. They pay no heed to his ardent pleas that he be left on the savage island.

The captain is one Pedro de Mendez, a Portuguese, and his ship is headed for Lisbon. He behaves with extreme civility towards Gulliver, offering the poor man food and clothing and a comfortable cabin. However, to the now demented Gulliver, Captain Mendez is only a Yahoo. Gulliver behaves sullenly. He confines himself to his cabin and even makes one attempt to throw himself overboard. He makes it clear to the captain that he fears defilement at the close approach of any of the crew or of the captain himself but, despite Gulliver's ungrateful behavior, the captain is able to see with great compassion that his passenger is mad and suffering greatly. He continues to behave decently and kindly towards Gulliver.

| Comment

So obsessed is he with his view of man as a Yahoo, that Gulliver is incapable of recognizing decency of a human kind and in a human being. Gulliver readily admits that Captain Mendez is kind and civil but he is, nevertheless, repelled by the Captain because he continues to see all men as Yahoos. Here, Gulliver is paradoxically committing the sin of pride because he is blind to human limitations, that is his madness. He is not impressed by the goodness of a good man because he has been dazzled by a vision of goodness which no man can attain. Thus, Gulliver has reached a point from which his reconciliation with human life seems most unlikely. He, in effect, hates even good men simply because even good men are not Houyhnhnms.

After an uneventful voyages, the ship arrives at Lisbon on November 5, 1715. The captain provides rooms for Gulliver in his house at Lisbon and gives the Englishman a suit of clothes which Gulliver airs out for twenty-four hours before wearing. The captain continues to treat Gulliver with patience and kindness; gradually, the poor man is eased back into human society. He peeps out of a window but withdraws in terror. In a few days, however, he is able to venture into the street although he must keep his nose stopped up with perfumes, so offensive to him are the smells of men.

Captain Mendez prevails upon his poor guest to consider returning to his family. Gulliver is reluctant to do so because, although his fear of people begins to diminish, his hatred and contempt for them increases. Nevertheless, he reconciles himself to rejoining his family and, on the fifth of December, 1715, he arrives at his home after a voyage from Lisbon.

His wife and family greet him with surprise and joy but the sight of them fills him with hatred, disgust and contempt. He is struck with shame and horror when he realizes that "by copulating with one of the yahoo species [he] had become a parent of more." Upon entering the house, he fell faint when his wife took him in her arms and kissed him. At the time of his writing this account of his return home, Gulliver had already been in England for five years and he tells us that he still has not permitted any of his family to touch his food or take him by the hand. For over a year after his arrival home, he did not permit any of his family into his presence, so disgusted was he by their smell. Even now, five years later, he spends most of his time in his stable, conversing with his horses whose smell is most agreeable to him.

CHAPTER XII

Here, Gulliver takes his leave of the reader. He takes the opportunity to emphasize that, unlike most travel books, his was written not to entertain or amuse with wild stories and fanciful lies, but, rather, with a single, clear purpose: to instruct. He advises the reader to take to heart the lessons to be learned from the glorious Houyhnhnms and the giant Brobdingnagians, the least corrupted of the Yahoo kind. He wishes also to defend himself against an accusation that has been brought against him: namely, that it never occurred to him to claim these far-flung lands as possessions of the English crown. He points out that the Lilliputians were not worth conquering while the Brobdingnagians, Laputians and Houyhnhnms were unconquerable. Furthermore, he disapproves of the barbaric cruelty perpetrated by a nation when it seeks to subjugate another people. He ironically confesses, however, that the English are not guilty of such practices.

Gulliver tells us that he will devote the remainder of his life to the lessons of virtue which he has learned among the Houyhnhnms and to instruct the Yahoos of his own family whenever they show themselves to be docile animals. "I began last week to permit my wife to sit at dinner with me, at the farthest end of a long table, and to answer (but with the utmost brevity) the few questions I asked her. Yet the smell of a Yahoo continuing very offensive I always keep my nose well stopt with rue, lavender or tobacco leaves. And although it be hard for a man late in life to remove old habits, I am not altogether out of hopes in some time to suffer a neighbor Yahoo in my company without the apprehensions I am yet under of his teeth or his claws."

Gulliver goes on to say that he is willing to accept the fact that Yahoos are dishonest, avaricious, wasteful, gluttonous and so on, but what makes it almost impossible for him to deal with these creatures, is that, in spite of all their obvious defects, they continue to be smitten with pride. "When I behold a lump of deformity and diseases, both in body and mind, smitten with pride, it immediately breaks all the measures of my patience." And, consequently, he concludes his book by warning all those who are in any way tainted with this vice of pride to remain forever out of his sight.

Comment

Swift's most masterful stroke of **irony** is seen in this conclusion. For we have before us a man inveighing with bitterness against the sin of pride but, in the very process of his attack on pride, Gulliver commits that same sin! For he sets himself up as a judge of humankind and he judges man on the basis of standards (Houyhnhnm standards) that are beyond the reach of men. Thus, if the Lilliputians were guilty of pride in their inability to see the difference between themselves and the giant Gulliver, Gulliver is guilty of the same sin in his apparent inability to reconcile himself to the fact that men are not Houyhnhnms. Man can attain only that degree of goodness that is attainable by an imperfect creature. True, most men are far from even this limited goal but Gulliver, in his dazzled madness, has failed to see that the goal is necessarily limited. He thus commits the sin he most hates and thereby proves how limited a creature is man.

ANALYSIS OF BOOK IV

In the first three books of the *Travels*, Swift has exposed to satiric ridicule the institutions, the customs, the beliefs and the behavior of man. In Book IV, however, he turns his attention to human nature itself. He seeks to discover what might be called a definition of man, a definition that will account for the apparent mess man has managed to make of his life and his world. Swift therefore places Gulliver (an ordinary mortal) directly between the figures of impossible perfection, the Houyhnhnms, and the figures of impossible degradation, the Yahoos. Gulliver is shaken to the core of his being when he suddenly sees, in the Yahoos, the terrible sight of man as animal. The Yahoos are images of what man would become were he totally devoid of reason and completely removed from civilization: they are images of the animal potential in man.

Stunned by the Yahoos, Gulliver makes the mistake of equating those brutes with men. In order to distinguish himself from these animals, he grows more and more attached to the Houyhnhnms who are images of absolute reason, a kind of reason quite different from human reason and, although he knows he cannot be a Houyhnhnm, Gulliver begins to judge mankind by Houyhnhnm standards. In the process, he grows alienated from his race and finds it unbearable to return to live among men.

The fact is, however, that man is neither Yahoo nor Houyhnhnm; he is an imperfect creature who, nevertheless, has the power to live a decent life if only he will recognize how limited he is. Swift presents us with figures like Count Munodi and Captain Mendez who are decent, compassionate, wise and humble men who have become aware of their capabilities only by recognizing their limitations. Without pride, these figures live the kind of good life attainable by humanity.

Gulliver, however, goes mad when he realizes that man is incapable of absolute perfection. Unable to come to terms with his limited capabilities, he thus commits the sin of pride as he is in the very process of condemning man for being proud. Ironically, Gulliver's madness ... his own pride ... proves how imperfect a creature man is. The tragedy is that, in the name of perfection, Gulliver misses the opportunity to achieve whatever goodness it is in his power to attain.

GULLIVER'S TRAVELS

CHARACTER ANALYSES

LEMUEL GULLIVER

The central figure in and narrator of *Gulliver's Travels*, is a good natured, hard-working, curious man, but a most ordinary one. He is subjected to most extraordinary experiences; some of these he understands, some he does not. When we first meet him, he amuses and bores us with his detailed accounts of the minutiae of his Lilliputian surroundings. We soon grow to admire him, however, as he shows himself to be kind, honorable and magnanimous in his dealings with the Lilliputians who, by contrast, are prideful, greedy and cruel. However, when Gulliver encounters the giants of Brobdingnag, he attempts to preserve his dignity as a man and as an English-man and, in the process, grows mean and contemptible in our eyes. In contrast to the giant King of Brobdingnag (who is a figure of common sense and kindness) Gulliver begins to appear as a figure of absurd pride as he attempts to win the respect of the King. In Book III, Gulliver again appears as a figure of humane common sense in relation to the absurd astronomers and projectors of Laputa and Lagado. Finally, in Book IV, we watch Gulliver as he is slowly driven mad by his realization that he can never hope to achieve the state of existence of the supremely rational, noble Houyhnhnms. We watch Gulliver discover a disturbing resemblance between himself and the odious yahoos and we watch him growing increasingly alienated from himself and the human race. We come to pity him as we realize that he falls victim to the same sin of pride which he condemns in others, the sin of failing to recognize and accept his limitations as a man. It is most important to our understanding of Swift's work that we recognize that Gulliver is not Swift.

Swift's meaning is created in the interplay between Gulliver and the reader but Swift has not made Gulliver an easy mouthpiece for his own views. The reader must divine Swift's meaning by analyzing Gulliver's responses to his experiences and some of those responses are not Swift's; some, of course, are but it is generally conceded that, where Gulliver functions merely as an obvious mouthpiece for Swift, as, for example, in certain parts of Book III, the **satire** is at its weakest.

THE LILLIPUTIAN EMPEROR

The Lilliputian Emperor can be seen, on one level, as an ironic depiction of King George I. The English reader would have smiled in encountering, in the Emperor, a figure whose physical features ... his handsomeness, his youth, his athletic agility ... were in marked and amusing contrast to the sluggish and boorish King George. On the other hand, the Emperor's love of military display and pageantry bear a direct resemblance to those features in King George's character and Swift is enjoying a joke at the King's expense. However, considered on a level other than that of direct political allegory, the Lilliputian Emperor is a figure of absurd pride and cruelty. He is an absolute monarch with unbounded ambitions and these features of his character are made to seem absurd in the light of his laughably insignificant physical stature. The Lilliputian Emperor embodies the political vices of tyranny, lust for power, and corrupt leadership.

FLIMNAP AND BOLGOLAM

Flimnap And Bolgolam are Swift's depiction of corrupt politicians. They are extremely envious and are given to constant intriguing. They conceive an immediate jealousy of Gulliver because of the favor he finds with the Emperor at first, a favor based upon his obvious usefulness to the state. Indeed, the more Gulliver does for Lilliput, the more envious do Flimnap and Bolgolam grow. Finally, they are able to launch a successful intrigue against Gulliver, forcing him to flee their country when, in fact, he could have been of such enormous service to that nation. Swift shows that intriguing politicians like Bolgolam and Flimnap have no real concern for their country. It is generally thought that Flimnap is a representation of Sir Robert Walpole, the Whig Prime Minister under George I, a man particularly despised by Swift.

THE BROBDINGNAGIAN FARMER

The Brobdingnagian Farmer in no way possesses moral qualities commensurate with his size. Although he is kind to Gulliver at first, he grows ruthlessly greedy in his exploitation of his prize as soon as he realizes that the little man can serve as a source of income. The Brobdingnagian farmer is blinded, by his greed and his size, to the sufferings of the weak and helpless Gulliver.

THE KING OF BROBDINGNAG

The King Of Brobdingnag is quite different from the farmer. He is a man of common sense and kindness and he embodies Swift's notion of a good king. He abhors the thought of exercising arbitrary and unlimited power over his subjects whose freedom he respects. He refuses, therefore, Gulliver's offer to provide him with gunpowder and cannons, believing that weapons of such cruelty, so capable of supporting a tyrant's lust for power, are best avoided. It is in contrast to the King of Brobdingnag that Gulliver begins to appear contemptible; the King, for all his size and strength, has a keen appreciation of the cruelty of the weapons Gulliver offers him while Gulliver, himself (so physically puny), is apparently unmoved by the suffering he shows these weapons to be capable of causing. The King of Brobdingnag is a liberally educated man and is not given to abstract speculation. Gulliver finds his refusal to accept gunpowder as the effects of "narrow principles and short views."

THE QUEEN OF BROBDINGNAG

The Queen Of Brobdingnag is a kind woman who is charmed by Gulliver and treats him with much affection as a kind of cute little pet. Gulliver gladly accepts the role she imposes upon him and goes out of his way to please her.

THE LAPUTAN KING

The Laputan King along with his mathematicians and astronomers, is an absurd, absent-minded individual, so given to abstract speculation that he cannot even carry on a conversation without being reminded by his servants that he must listen and speak. These people are cut off from real life; their wives despise them and take every opportunity to escape the dreary existence imposed upon them.

THE PROJECTORS OF LAGADO

The Projectors Of Lagado attempt to apply the abstract learning of the Laputian scientists to the practical affairs of life. As Swift depicts them, they seem to be madmen engaged in useless schemes which never work. Wherever their schemes are applied, the land is barren and the people wretchedly poor. Instead of using the traditional wisdom of the past, these projectors bring ruin upon their land by insisting upon experimenting with new methods.

COUNT MUNODI

Unlike the projectors, Count Munodi is a man of common sense who is glad to make use of the best ideas and methods inherited from the past. Thanks to his common sense and wisdom, his estate is in a flourishing condition: his mansion is a beautiful building and his farm is productive. He is, however, despised by the projectors who pressure him to use their methods. He finds it increasingly difficult to resist their pressure and gloomily foresees the ruin of his estate and his way of life.

THE STRULDBRUGGS

The Struldbruggs are the unfortunate beings who are doomed to eternal life. However, since they are not blessed with eternal youth, they are in a state of perpetual decay. Gulliver is horrified at their sight and they, therefore, constitute for him an object lesson in the foolishness of the human desire for immortality. Gulliver comes to understand that death can be a blessing and that the problem for a human being is to live as well as he can in his allotted span rather than to hanker after an immortality which would be just as much a curse as it is an impossibility.

THE HOUYHNHNMS

The Houyhnhnms are creatures of absolute rationality who happen to inhabit the bodies of horses. Gulliver is dazzled by their freedom from passion, envy, hatred and greed. He fails to understand that their way of life is simply impossible for human beings who are not constituted as are the Houyhnhnms. The Houyhnhnms, while unaffected by the pain which men suffer on account of their passions, are similarly untouched by the joy which can sometimes come to men through their passions. The Houyhnhnms cultivate friendship but it is a cold kind of friendship, unmarked by the strong personal attachments which are present in the closest of human connections. The Houyhnhnms are good parents but they are not passionately involved with their offspring; any Houyhnhnm can serve as the parent to any Houyhnhnm "child" and often does. The life of the Houyhnhnms is unmarked by discord or even disagreement; since they all have reason (and reason, for them, is not a means of argument but an immediate insight into truth) they need have no discussions since they are inevitably in agreement on all but the most insignificant issues. So dazzled is he by the admirable features of Houyhnhnm life that Gulliver does not realize how grim an existence their life would be for a human being who does not possess the same kind of reason they own.

THE YAHOOS

The Yahoos are the most striking figures in Swift's masterpiece. They are odious, smelly, filthy brutes who (upon close examination) are seen to bear a remarkable resemblance to human beings. They are greedy, quarrelsome and cruel and are constantly at each other's throats. Gulliver is mortified to recognize their physical resemblance to him and he assumes that there is a corresponding moral resemblance as well. The Yahoos have no trace of reason and serve the Houyhnhnms in the same fashion as horses and oxen serve farmers in England.

    Concerning the Yahoos, the chief question to be considered is that of their function in the book as representations of man. Does Swift mean us to draw the same conclusions that Gulliver draws: namely, that the Yahoos are men and men are Yahoos? There is no easy answer to this problem but it seems clear that the Yahoos, odious as they are, do not simply represent man but represent what man can become if he does not exercise properly that small quantity of reason which is his. The Yahoos, it must be remembered, are creatures removed from society and civilization. Swift hints that their ancestry can be traced back to two original, stranded humans who appeared on Houyhnhnmland one day ages ago. Thus removed from human society, their decline into brutes was inevitable. However, if the Yahoo represents what man can become when he abjures reason and gives himself over wholly to his appetites and passions, Swift introduces an ironic and bitter twist into his treatment of man and Yahoo in Book IV for he suggests that, in a sense even civilized man is worse than the disgusting Yahoo. After all, civilized has some portion of that reason which the Yahoo utterly lacks and yet he has generally used that reason not to procure for himself the good life but, rather, to intensify the destructive and degenerate tendencies at the heart of his nature. As are most of the things in this book, Swift's Yahoos are complex figures whose meaning, perhaps, is not available to capsule-style exposition.

CAPTAIN PEDRO DE MENDEZ

Captain Pedro De Mendez plays a small role in *Gulliver's Travels* but a very important one for he is Gulliver's first human contact after his two years on Houyhnhnmland and his response to Mendez is indicative of what has happened to him in those two years. Mendez is extraordinarily kind and patient to Gulliver; he recognizes that his strange passenger has been deranged but he does what he can to make Gulliver's return to human society as painless as possible. Captain Mendez shows what is, perhaps, the most important human virtue, charity. However, the unfortunate Gulliver, although he recognizes that Mendez is a good man, continues to respond to him as if he were a Yahoo. In other words, he has been so blinded by his experience on Houyhnhnmland that he is now incapable of responding to such human goodness as he does encounter. Gulliver continues to see Captain Mendez as a Yahoo although the good captain certainly shows more kindness to the unfortunate madman than did the noble Houyhnhnms.

GULLIVER'S TRAVELS

CRITICAL COMMENTARY

THE QUESTION OF SWIFT'S MISANTHROPY

Gulliver's Travels was enthusiastically received when it was published in 1726 but it was, by its very nature, subject to serious misunderstanding. It was not long before readers and critics began to confuse Gulliver's attitude towards man with Swift's attitude. The result was that Swift was often attacked as some sort of perverted misanthrope. Only a diseased and malevolent mind it was said, could have conceived of such a creature as the Yahoo as a **metaphor** for man. In support of this contention, much was made of the story that Swift apparently was insane during the last few years of his life. Probably, the most notable exponent of this view of the Dean and of his book was William Thackeray, the great English novelist of the nineteenth century.

RECENT ATTITUDES TOWARDS THE HOUYHNHNMS AND YAHOOS

It such an interpretation of *Gulliver's Travels* is misguided it must nevertheless, be admitted that an understanding of the

Houyhnhnms and Yahoos is crucial to an understanding of *Gulliver's Travels*. This, however, is no easy matter. In fact, it is not surprising that Book IV of *the Travels* has attracted more critical attention than any other aspect of Swift's work, particularly in recent years.[2] A good deal of thought to on this subject was stimulated by the appearance of Professor Irvin Ehrenpreis' article on the Houyhnhnms in which he contended that Swift was satirizing the deists in his depiction of the Houyhnhnms.[3] Ehrenpreis argued that the Houyhnhnms represented an attitude toward life which Swift detested. This position was quickly attacked by an number of notable scholars (especially Professor Sherburn) who argued that, although the Houyhnhnms were certainly not to be taken as models for human imitation, they, nevertheless, represented ideals to which Swift subscribed.[4] Ehrenpreis has since modified his original view but the world of Swift scholarship is indebted to him for having stimulated much thought on an important subject which still remains perhaps the most crucial issue of Swift's work. Other significant work on Book IV includes Roland M. Frye's study of the Yahoos[5] in which he shows that Swift has represented these figures of degenerate humanity within the system of Christian symbolism of sin. A particularly illuminating discussion of Book IV is to be found in Professor S. H. Monk's article, "The Pride of Lemuel Gulliver" which draws together the experiences of Gulliver in the first three books and interprets the meaning of Book IV in the light of the first three books.[6] Indeed, the interpretive comments in this review book are indebted, in many places, to Professor Monk's insights. Professor Monk's article analyzes brilliantly the shifting role of Gulliver himself in each of his voyages and, from the standpoint of Gulliver's position, analyzes the meaning of the Houyhnhnms and Yahoos. If there may be said to be a consensus among Swift scholars concerning the meaning of Houyhnhnms and Yahoo, that consensus would disagree with Ehrenpreis' contention that Swift attacks the Houyhnhnms but would stop short of suggesting that Swift meant man to imitate the Houyhnhnm. Professor Monk's article shows clearly why man cannot imitate the Houyhnhnms. The student who wishes to read the best that has been written on this problem should consult *A Casebook on Gulliver among the Houyhnhnms*, edited by Milton Foster.[7] This is a collection of essays on this topic which is so crucial to an understanding of Swift. All of the above mentioned articles, and many more, are included in Foster's collection.

STUDIES OF SWIFT'S SATIRIC TECHNIQUE

Swift criticism since the war has been particularly successful in illuminating not only the **themes** with which the author was occupied but also the techniques through which he expressed those **themes** and concerns. Indeed, it might be maintained that more work has been devoted to Swift's satiric technique in the last twenty years than had been in the two hundred years immediately after Swift's death. Particularly important have been the insights gained into Swift's use of **irony**. W. B. Ewald has demonstrated how Swift's **irony** is developed from the "persona" (or mask) the author assumes in each of his works;[8] that is, only by recognizing and analyzing the character and position of the narrator the author creates as his mouthpiece, can the reader understand what Swift is attacking and how he attacks it. Ewald has shown that, in each of his works, Swift has used a highly individualized mask suitable to his satiric purpose in that work. John M. Bullitt has investigated the technique of **satire** from still another point of view, that of the rhetorical processes involved in the satiric mode.[9] He has tried to show how Swift manipulates language, character, and situation in order to create **satire**; and he has shown how Swift's satiric effects can lead to tragic (and comic) conclusions. Two other recent and valuable studies of the literary art in Swift's **satire** are Martin Price's *Swift's Rhetorical Art* and Herbert Davis' *The **Satire** of Jonathan Swift*. In addition to book length studies, any number of articles have been written on Swift's satiric techniques; worthy of special attention are F. R. Leavis' "The **Irony** of Swift," and Ricardo Quintana's "Situational Satire."[10]

BIOGRAPHICAL STUDIES OF SWIFT

Interest in Swift, however, has by no means been limited to the literary aspects of his career. Biographical interest in Swift has always been lively but, unfortunately, not always fruitful. A good deal of fanciful speculation, based upon irresponsible psychologizing, has passed for biography since Swift's death. The best prewar biography of Swift is by Emile Pons but it covers only Swift's early life.[11] Since the war, however, a number of biographies have appeared each of which has its own merits. Most notable are John Middleton Murry's *Jonathan Swift; Critical Biography*, and Professor Ehrenpreis' study *Swift: The Man, His Works and the Age*, of which the first of three volumes has appeared. Ehrenpreis' work combines rigorous scholarly investigation and perceptive literary interpretation. He is scrupulously careful to avoid involvement with the more fanciful legends about Swift, those legends that have, unfortunately, comprised too much of the concern of many of Swift's biographers. In addition to these general biographies, several excellent shorter studies have appeared on Swift's life and work as a churchman and an Irishman. Of these, Louis Landa's *Swift and the Church of Ireland*. Philip Harth's *Swift and Anglican* Rationalism, and Oliver Ferguson's *Jonathan Swift and Ireland* are particularly noteworthy. In summation, we may say that biographical interest in Swift has recently been evident in works of serious and responsible scholarship rather than in fanciful psychologizing. Swift is becoming more of a man and less of a legend and, in the process, his fascination grows. Also deserving attention in this context is Ehrenpreis' shorter work, *The Personality of Jonathan Swift*, which is not a biography but, rather, a collection of short studies of Swift's work approached through the Dean's biography. It is in this collection of studies that Ehrenpreis' previously mentioned interpretation of the meaning of the Houyhnhnms appeared.

It is clear that critical and biographical material on Swift is available in great abundance. In this short summary, it has been possible to suggest only superficially the extent and depth of the work that has been done on Swift and to indicate the nature of the major concerns with and approaches to that author. The serious students would be wise to consult the annual bibliographies of literary scholarship to be found in *Philological Quarterly* and *PMLA* if he wishes to become more fully acquainted with the range, of Swift scholarship and, of special help, is Louis Landa's biography of the scholarship of Swift produced from 1900 to 1945. A supplement to this bibliography is also available, carrying the list into the 1950. A detailed but hardly all inclusive list of critical and biographical studies follows in this review book.

FOOTNOTES

1. William Makepeace Thackeray, *English Humorists of the Eighteenth Century*, 1853.

2. Merrel D. Clubb, "The Criticism of Gulliver's 'Voyage to Houyhnhnms' 1726–1914," Stanford *Studies in Language and Literature*, ed. H. Craig 1941, pp. 203-32.

3. Irving Ehrenpreis, *The Personality of Jonathan Swift*, 1958.

4. George Sherburn, "Errors Concerning the Houyhnhnms," *Modern Philology*, November, 1958, pp. 92–92. See also Louis Landa, "A Note on Irvin Ehrenpreis' The Personality of Jonathan Swift," *Philological Quarterly* July 1959, pp. 351–352.

5. Roland M. Frye, "Swift's Yahoos and the Christian Symbols for Sin," *Journal of the History of* Ideas, April, 1954, pp. 201–217.

6. Samuel H. Monk, "The Pride of Lemuel Gulliver," *Sewanee Review Winter* 1955, pp. 48–71.

7. *A Casebook on Gulliver among the Houyhnhnms*, ed. Milton Foster. Thomas Y. Crowell, 1961.

8. W.B. Ewald Jr., *The Masks of Jonathan Swift*, 1954.

9. see *Scrutiny*, March, 1934, pp. 364–78.

10. see *University of Toronto Quarterly*, January, 1948, pp. 130–36.

11. Emile Pons, *Swift: les Anees de Jeuenesse et le 'Conte de Tonneau'*, 1925.

GULLIVER'S TRAVELS

STUDY GUIDE
ESSAY QUESTIONS AND ANSWERS

Question: How does the political corruption of the Lilliputian government reflect the moral defects of the Lilliputian people?

Answer: In Book I, Swift depicts a society which is politically corrupt and traces the roots of that political corruption back to the basic moral defect of the Lilliputians, their pride. The Lilliputian's Emperor is an absolute monarch. Since all power rests in his hands, his subjects are forced to abandon their dignity as men in order to win advancement in his court. Their advancement is not based upon considerations of merit but upon their willingness to submit to the Emperor's power. They are rewarded for their ability to dance on a rope or to climb above and creep under a stick which is raised or lowered at the Emperor's bidding; to us (the readers) it is clear that their willingness to dance on ropes and creep under sticks is a sign of their willingness to be corrupted, to give up their dignity in the name of political reward. In other words, the political system of Lilliput, because it is based upon the absolute power of one man, is necessarily corrupt and we see how a corrupt system breeds corrupt men. Now, if we trace the course of this political corruption back to the moral nature of the Lilliputians, we find that it is the pride of the Emperor (his blindness to his limitations) which leads him to the pursuit of absolute power. This is especially evident in his desire to subjugate completely his Blefuscudian foes, an ambition which horrifies Gulliver and which, to us, seems pathetically ridiculous in the light of the diminutive stature of the Emperor. Thus, the Emperor's thirst for unlimited power makes him an absolute ruler and his absolute rule gives rise to a government which is necessarily corrupt. Furthermore, the Emperor's desire for unlimited power is a symptom of his pride, or his blindness to his own limitations.

Question: How does Swift use the figure of Gulliver in Book II as a means of involving the reader in the satiric attack on mankind?

Answer: In Book I, Gulliver is not only much larger than the tiny Lilliputians; he is also much better than they are. The reader tends to identify with Gulliver and to come away from Book I with his faith in humanity well supported. This is because the reader tends to see Gulliver (and not the Lilliputians) as the representative of mankind in Book I and Gulliver is shown to be kind, patient, and humble.

Having confirmed the reader's good opinion for himself, Swift, in Book II, springs his satiric trap. Gulliver is placed in an environment which challenges his very conception of himself as a man: in the land of the giants where a tabletop is as large as a baseball field, where a six-month infant can handle him like a toy, where a rat is a terrifying beast, Gulliver struggles valiantly to retain his dignity as a man and to convince the giants of Brobdingnag that he deserves to be taken seriously as a human being. Now the reader cannot help identifying with Gulliver in his plight; but, as Gulliver tries harder and harder to impress the mighty giants, he begins to appear pathetic and ignoble; pathetic, because he is clearly faced with an impossible task. He is, after all, puny compared with the giants and he becomes ridiculous as he strives to impress them. He is ignoble because, in trying to impress the king of Brobdingnag with English life and government, he becomes the spokesman for institutions and behavior which are corrupt and cruel but he tries to gloss over their corruption and cruelty. In other words, because he cannot accept the consequences of being insectisized in a land of giants, Gulliver tries to show that he is as good as a giant. That is to say, in Brobdingnag, Gulliver behaves towards the giants as the Lilliputians had behaved towards him. In this hostile environment, he is shown to be as prideful, corrupt and cruel as were the Lilliputians.

Now, for the reader, Gulliver's behavior presents a difficult problem. On the one hand, the reader recognizes that Gulliver is behaving poorly in Brobdingnag; on the other hand, the reader sympathizes with Gulliver and understands the predicament which forces him to behave ignobly. The reader, after all, is human and shares with Gulliver the need to preserve his dignity against the challenge offered to it by the giants and their giant-sized land. The effect, then, of Book II is to question seriously the reader's high opinion of humanity and to suggest that man is a good deal more complex a creature than any simply optimistic view of human nature would indicate. For we see that, even reasonably good men like Gulliver (and not only Lilliputians) are smitten by pride. Indeed, it seems that pride is that element in our makeup which defines us as men! By forcing the reader to identify with and (at the same time) criticize Gulliver, Swift has forced the reader to discover this defect in his own nature.

Question: Why did Swift unleash so strong an attack against science and what alternatives to the scientific approach to life does he consider to be available to man?

Answer: What most bothered Swift about science and scientists was that the endeavor to discover the natural causes of natural phenomena was not a morally significant venture. This is an old idea in traditional Christian thought but it is an idea that was going out of fashion as science became more and more important a feature of western life. Swift left that scientific knowledge had no necessary connection with the moral quality of one's life. Thus, he shows us that the Laputians, those supreme scientists, are entirely cut off from real life: they cannot converse with each other, so lost are they in thought; their wives despise them and seek only to escape them; and their knowledge of mathematics, astronomy and music does not even guarantee that their clothes will fit them.

The reason why science could have no moral importance for man was that science, it seemed to Swift, was an endeavor that depended entirely on the human intellect. Thus, he shows us the "projectors" in Book III trying to apply scientific principles to the solution of human problems and failing miserably. Swift's point is that human problems, which are moral problems, cannot be solved by the mere exercise of reason. In effect, the scientists and projectors are guilty of intellectual pride, of failing to understand the limitations of the unaided human mind.

Now, in the figure of Count Munodi, Swift presents us with an alternative to the scientific approach to life. Count Munodi's home and estate are in dramatic contrast to the disordered and barren homes and fields built and tended by the projectors. The reason (according to Swift) for the order, beauty and productivity of the Count's estate is to be found in his attitude towards the solution of architectural and agricultural problems. Count Munodi depends heavily upon the accumulated wisdom of the past: he makes use of the best of the styles of the past; he uses the tested agricultural methods of the past. He makes use of traditional wisdom because he recognizes that man's intellect alone is not enough to deal with all of man's problems.

Whether Swift correctly evaluated, understood and represented the procedures and purposes of science is an open question. In Book III, however, he uses science as a **metaphor** for man's search for unnecessary knowledge and man's tendency to overlook the limitations of his intellect.

Question: Discuss the figure of the Houyhnhnms and Yahoos in Book III as they point up the predicament of man.

Answer: Swift's purpose in writing *Gulliver's Travels* was to provide man with some conception of the good life but the "good life" is meant to be lived and, if it is to be lived, it must be within the realm of human capability. Therefore, one way of regarding *Gulliver's Travels* is as an attempt to provide a definition of man; exactly what is man and what is he not? If we know this much, then we know what is in the realm of human capability and our conception of the good life can become a practical guide for man.

Now, to Gulliver, man is apparently defined by the Yahoo, an odious, filthy, greedy, tormented brute, without reason. The Yahoo, Gulliver is shocked to discover, bears a close physical resemblance to man but is totally animalistic in behavior. In effect, then, Gulliver sees in the Yahoo a reduced image of man, man as animal-and Swift makes every attempt to call our attention to the possibilities of physical disgust in such an image of man. We, and Gulliver, are repelled by the Yahoo but Gulliver is particularly affected by the beast since he makes the mistake of identifying the Yahoo with man.

In direct contrast to the Yahoo, is the Houyhnhnm, a remarkable creature who embodies (in the shape of a horse) the quality of absolute reason. Gulliver begins to love and admire the Houyhnhnms but he makes the mistake of evaluating human conduct on the basis of Houyhnhnm standards. Swift makes it very clear, however, that Houyhnhnm reason is beyond the reach of even the best of men. Seen through Houyhnhnm eyes, therefore, man appears even worse than the Yahoos for he has made bad use of his small faculty of reason while the Yahoos had no reason at all.

However, are Houyhnhnm standards the correct standards for man? Gulliver acts as if they were and goes mad when he realizes that man cannot hope to become a Houyhnhnm. In effect, Gulliver is committing the sin of pride because he is overlooking the limits of human capability in judging man by standards inapplicable to him. The real question raised by Book IV, the real human predicament, is this: how is man to become better than a Yahoo if it is impossible for him to be a Houyhnhnm? Gulliver does not ask this question but rather assumes that, because man cannot be a Houyhnhnm, he must be Yahoo.

There is no easily stated answer to the predicament involved in attempting to overcome Yahoo potential. The answer must be sought in the book as a whole but the beginning of an answer is evident in the attitude with which Swift has approached his book. Throughout, he has shown that man is a very complex creature; he is not naturally good but he does not have to be hopelessly bad. He must recognize his limitations if he is to be aware of those capabilities which, in fact, he does possess. He must accept whatever help is available from religion, from society and from tradition in his attempt to lead the good life. He must recognize that the good life is not, for man, a perfect life but that it is an endurable one; and, if these observations seem not to be revolutionary or original, Swift would answer that the truth is not likely to be a novelty although the truth can be ignored. *Gulliver's Travels* was written, indeed, because Swift believed that his world was becoming blind to these truths which had once been the basis of the moral life of man.

BIBLIOGRAPHY AND TOPICS FOR THE RESEARCH

BIBLIOGRAPHY

A. *The Eighteenth Century Background: Literature, History, Thought* Butt, John. *The Augustan Age*, 1950.

Cassirer, Ernst. *The Philosophy of the Enlightenment*, 1951.

Clark, G. N. *The Latter Stuarts*, 1660–1714, (1934). Oxford History of England.

Eighteen Century English Literature: Modern Essays in Criticism, ed. James L. Clifford. Oxford: Galaxy Books, 1959.

Gallaway, Francis. *Reason, Rule and Revolt in English Classicism*, 1940.

Jones, R. F. *Ancients and Moderns*, 1936.

Nicolson, Marjorie H. *Newton Demands the Muse*, 1946.

Nicolson, Marjorie H. *Voyages to the Moon*, 1948.

Nicolson, Marjorie H. *Science and Imagination*, 1956.

Sherburn, George. *The Eighteenth Century in A Literary History of England*, ed. A. C. Baugh et al, 1948.

Willey, Basil. *The Eighteenth Century Background*, 1940.

Williams, Basil. *The Whig Supremacy*, 1714–1760, (1939). Oxford History of England.

B. *Biographies and Biographical Studies of Swift*

Ehrenpreis, Irvin. *Swift: the Man, the Works, the Age*. Vol. I. Cambridge, Mass. 1962.

Ehrenpreis, Irvin. *The Personality of Jonathan Swift*, 1958.

Ferguson, Oliver. *Jonathan Swift and Ireland*, 1962.

Jackson, Robert Wyse. *Jonathan Swift: Dean and Pastor*, 1939.

Landa, Louis L. *Swift and the Church of Ireland*, 1962.

Murry, John Middleton. *Jonathan Swift: a Critical Biography*, 1954.

Van Doren, Carl. *Jonathan Swift*, 1930.

C. *General Studies of Swift*

Brown, James. "Swift as Moralist," *Philological Quarterly*, October 1945, pp. 368–87.

Jefferson, D. W. "An Approach to Swift," in *From Dryden to Johnson*, ed. Boris Ford (Pelican Guide to English Literature), 1957.

Quintana, Ricardo. *Swift: an Introduction*, 1955.

Quintana, Ricardo. *The Mind and Art of Jonathan Swift*, 1936, 1953.

Williams, Kathleen. *Jonathan Swift and the Age of Compromise*, 1958.

D. *Studies of Swift's Satiric Technique.*

Bullitt, John M. *Jonathan Swift and the Anatomy of **Satire***, 1953.

Davis, Herbert. *The **Satire** of Jonathan Swift*, 1947.

Ewald, W. B., Jr. *The Masks of Jonathan Swift*, 1954.

Leavis, F. R. "The **Irony** of Swift," *Scrutiny*, March 1934, pp. 364–78.

Price, Martin. *Swift's Rhetorical Art: a Study in Structure and Meaning*, 1953.

Quintana, R. "Situational Satire," *University of Toronto Quarterly*, January 1948, pp. 130–36.

Redinger, Ruby. "Jonathan Swift, the Disenchanter," *American Scholar*, Spring 1946, pp. 221–26.

Sams, Henry W. "Swift's **Satire** of the Second Person," *ELH*, March 1959, pp. 36–44.

E. *Studies of Gulliver's Travels*

Case, Arthur E. *Four Essays on Gulliver's Travels*, 1945.

Fink, Z. S. "Political Theory in Gulliver's Travels," *ELH*, June, 1947, pp. 151–61.

Frye, Roland M. "Swift's Yahoos and the Christian Symbols for Sin, *Journal of the History of* Ideas, April 1954, pp. 201–17.

Jones, R. F. "The Background of the Attack on Science in the Age of Pope," in *Eighteenth Century English Literature*, ed. J. L. Clifford Oxford: Galaxy Books, 1959.

Monk, S. H. "The Pride of Lemuel Gulliver," *Sewanee Review*, Winter, 1955, pp. 48–71. Also, in *Eighteenth Century English Literature*, ed. Clifford. (See note above.)

Potter, George R. "Swift and Natural Science," *Philological Quarterly*, January, 1941, pp. 97–118.

Ross, John F. "The 'Final Comedy of Lemuel Gulliver," *University of California Studies*, 1941, pp. 175–96.

Sherburn, George. "Errors Concerning the Houyhnhnms," *Modern Philology*, November 1958, pp. 92–97.

Stone, Edward. "Swift and the Horses: Misanthropy or Comedy?" *Modern Language Quarterly*, September 1949, pp. 367–76.

Sutherland, John H. "A Reconsideration of Gulliver's Third Voyage," *Studies in Philology*, January 1957, pp. 45–52.

Wedel, T. O. "The Philosophical Background of Gulliver's Travels," *Studies in Philology*, October 1926, pp. 434–50.

Note: Most of the important articles on the difficult voyage to Houyhnhnmland are collected in *A Casebook on Gulliver among the Houyhnhnms*, ed. Milton Foster. Thomas Y. Crowell Co.: New York, 1961. (Paper). This valuable collection contains some of the articles listed above.

F. Useful Reading in Works Earlier than and Contemporary with Swift

Addison and Steele. *The Spectator*.

Cervantes. *Don Quixote*.

Dryden, John. *Absalom and Achitophel.*

Pope, Alexander. *The Dunciad.*

Pope, Alexander. *An Essay on Man.*

Rabelais. *Gargantua and Pantagruel.*

Mandeville, Bernard. *The Fable of the Bees.*

Shaftesbury, Earl of. *Characteristics.*

TOPICS FOR THE RESEARCH AND CRITICAL PAPER

Swift's involvement with English politics, 1708-1715.

Swift as Churchman and Irish patriot, 1720-1736.

England under the Tories, 1710-1715.

Political Allegory in *Gulliver's Travels.*

Swift's attitude towards religion as expressed in the Voyage to Lilliput.

A comparison of the King of Brobdingnag and the Emperor of Lilliput.

An analysis of Swift's use of size in Books I and II.

The role of Gulliver.

The meaning of Gulliver's madness.

Swift's attitude toward science as expressed in Book III.

An analysis of Count Munodi.

The use of **irony** in *Gulliver's Travels*.

The changing meaning of the word "reason" in *Gulliver's Travels*.

Education of the young in Houyhnhnmland and Brobdingnag.

An analysis of the Houyhnhnms as symbols of absolute reason.

The Houyhnhnms; their virtues and defects.

The Yahoo as a symbol of man.

A comparison of *Gulliver's Travels* and a modern **satire** (*Animal Farm* or *1984*).

www.ingramcontent.com/pod-product-compliance
Lightning Source LLC
LaVergne TN
LVHW021709060526
838200LV00050B/2580